PRAISE FOR JIM WALLIS AND
REDISCOVERING **VALUES**

"One of America's most thoughtful, provocative, and powerful prophetic voices does it again. With moral incisiveness expressed in terms accessible to all, Wallis impressively weaves together economic theory, corporate realities, cultural analysis, and religious values to put a human face on, and bring moral clarity to, our economic crisis. His delineation of the responsibilities of corporate America ought to be studied in every corporation and business school. Religious leaders of any faith looking to address the corporate responsibility in our economic crisis will find no more eloquent, incisive, or morally powerful guide than *Rediscovering Values*."

—David Saperstein, director and counsel of
Religious Action Center of Reform Judaism

"Wallis is the most influential and visionary religious leader of our time. His broad appeal and impact are reminiscent of Reinhold Niebuhr and Martin Luther King Jr. Not only has he provided clear intellectual direction for our political, cultural, and spiritual renaissance, he has launched a movement to renew the church and our democracy."

—Robert M. Franklin, president of Morehouse College and author of
Crisis in the Village: Restoring Hope in African American Communities

"At this critical time in history, Jim Wallis offers a guidebook for all who long to reflect wisely on our personal and corporate choices and return to true biblical values that offer hope to this broken world."   —Lynne Hybels, advocate for Global Engagement,
Willow Creek Community Church

"Is it possible to change the world's trajectory? Can we create a new moral compass in the aftermath of the recent economic crisis? In *Rediscovering Values*, Jim Wallis argues that the world can change when people of good faith make different choices and act collectively. Read this book and join the movement—Jim calls us, as Jesus did, to challenge the status quo by making 'kingdom' choices." —Rich Stearns, president of World Vision US and author of *The Hole in Our Gospel*

"Could it be that today's problems will actually bring benefit beyond mere solutions? Jim Wallis leads us to the foundational values that will not only improve our circumstances but build our character." —Dr. Joel C. Hunter, senior pastor of Northland: A Church Distributed

"Agree or disagree—Jim Wallis touches your heart, stretches your mind, and challenges your values. He thunders like an Old Testament prophet, yet he is gentle and gracious. With a heart for people and a dream for a better tomorrow, Jim Wallis looks tough times in the eye and talks of hope." —Leith Anderson, president of National Association of Evangelicals

"Jim Wallis challenges us to focus on important societal issues from the standpoint of his theological faith beliefs. He is a consistent advocate of the idea that if we are to take Christ's teachings seriously, we must engage in issues of poverty and justice." —Jonathan T. M. Reckford, CEO of Habitat for Humanity International

REDISCOVERING
VALUES

REDISCOVERING
VALUES

A GUIDE FOR ECONOMIC
AND MORAL RECOVERY

JIM WALLIS

HOWARD BOOKS
A DIVISION OF SIMON & SCHUSTER, INC.
New York • Nashville • London • Toronto • Sydney

Published by Howard Books, a division of Simon & Schuster, Inc.
1230 Avenue of the Americas, New York, NY 10020
www.howardpublishing.com

Rediscovering Values © 2010, 2011 by Jim Wallis

In association with the literary agency of Jan Miller,
Dupree Miller & Associates

First Howard Books trade paperback edition February 2011

HOWARD and colophon are registered trademarks of
Simon & Schuster, Inc.

For information regarding special discounts for bulk purchases,
please contact Simon & Schuster Special Sales at 1-866-506-1949
or business@simonandschuster.com.

The Simon & Schuster Speakers Bureau can bring authors to your live event.
For more information or to book an event, contact the Simon & Schuster
Speakers Bureau at 1-866-248-3049 or visit our website at
www.simonspeakers.com.

Manufactured in the United States of America

10   9   8   7   6   5   4   3   2

Library of Congress Cataloging-in-Publication Data is available.

ISBN 978-1-4391-8312-0
ISBN 978-1-4391-8319-9 (pbk)
ISBN 978-1-4391-8317-5 (ebook)

*This book is dedicated to my sons, Luke (eleven)
and Jack (six). They make me laugh, they make me proud,
they give me good ideas, their social conscience challenges my own,
their indignation at what is wrong makes me more willing
to challenge the status quo, their prayers every night help shape
my faith, and the choices we make about the issues
raised in this book will determine their future.*

ACKNOWLEDGMENTS

This book, like all books, was made possible by more people than just the author.

The person I have most to thank is Tim King, my special assistant and now communications manager, who fervently believed there was a book in the things I was feeling and saying on the road about the economic crisis and the values it both revealed and called for. Tim travels with me, and as one of the best new leaders in the next faith-inspired generation, he is also convinced that a moral recovery should accompany the economic one, and that his contemporaries are eager to learn the lessons of the Great Recession. Tim spent countless hours doing research for this book, and we shaped it together.

Duane Shank, my longtime collaborator and friend, also helped with research and editing and brought years of experience into the mix. Duane is the master editor on my book projects. Joan Bisset, my chief administrator, found ways to build time to write into an already much too busy schedule, kept the project moving along, deadlines in front of us, and always kept the end goal in mind. Chuck Gutenson, Sojourners' chief operating officer, helped keep the organization running smoothly while I was writing. Every day, the committed and competent Sojourners staff inspires me with examples of the values at the heart of this book. A special thank-you goes to my friend Chester Spencer, one of D.C.'s best cabdrivers, who always gets me where I need to go and is a valued member of our team. One morning, Chester was the one who finally came up with the best configuration of the words for the title and subtitle of this book.

The Simon & Schuster team's enthusiastic belief in this book helped to keep me going on a greatly accelerated schedule. Jonathan Merkh and Becky Nesbitt were role models of what a publisher and editor are supposed to be, Philis Boultinghouse improved the book with her editing and made sure we had an on-time finished manuscript for the printer, and Jennifer Willingham was both creative and adamant about getting the book's message out.

As always, my wife and life partner, Joy Carroll, was a reliable source of both feedback and encouragement. I always want to know what Joy thinks. And my sons, Luke and Jack, had lots of ideas for me and showed wonderful patience for the time that writing takes—as long as I continued to prioritize coaching both of their Little League teams!

And this book simply would not have happened if my agent, Jan Miller, and her right-hand coworker Shannon Marven hadn't passionately believed in it and created the publishing solutions to make it possible.

The quiet times of writing each morning, before Joy and the kids get up, were both contemplative and productive about the deep moral issues of this economic crisis, teaching me that we had to go deeper to find our way out and the way forward.

CONTENTS

CONTENTS

REDISCOVERING
VALUES

INTRODUCTION

A GUIDE FOR ECONOMIC AND MORAL RECOVERY

Let's get personal. My brother's home is underwater in Detroit. Sadly, most of us now know what "underwater" means—that the house a family owns has dropped so much in value that it is worth less than the mortgage they still owe on it. You can't afford to sell the house, so you can't move. And that is a problem for Bill and Tess and many others, because Detroit doesn't have enough police to protect the city anymore and the cops can't respond to house alarms until *the next day.* So in my brother's neighborhood, and many others, people are breaking into homes to rob them with impunity, casually stripping the places because they know they have lots of time. It's scary.

And my brother's job is getting more difficult each day. He manages one of the largest social service organizations in Detroit, trying to take care of the most vulnerable in the city—from the forgotten elderly to at-risk kids. But in this economic climate, Bill's organizational funding is continually cut, and more and more people are falling between the cracks. My brother's everyday problem: Increasing numbers of people are in need, but he has fewer resources to meet those needs. So Bill has to cut his staff, then go home and worry about his own family's safety. His kids are in college and working on the other side of the state, and Bill sadly hopes they don't ever come back to Detroit.

It has been more than two years since the Great Recession hit hard. What have we learned? How have we changed? Is there any progress to report? Last year, when *Rediscovering Values* first came out, I said the right question was not just "When will the crisis end?" but "How will this crisis change us?" One year later, we are still struggling to answer that fundamental question.

On Wall Street, where this financial crisis began, record profits are being reported. The number of millionaires in New York grew more than 18 percent between 2008 and 2009, surpassing pre-recession levels and totaling more than 650,000. Another high-growth area for millionaires? Greater Washington, D.C. The number of people joining the seven-figure ranks climbed even more rapidly, at 19 percent, also passing the 2007 levels.

At the same time, the U.S. Census Bureau discovered that the number of people living in poverty increased to its highest level in fifty-one years, 43.6 million people. One in five American children now live in poverty. And while unemployment remains stubbornly at about 10 percent, those included on *Forbes* magazine's list of the four hundred richest Americans in 2010 saw an 8 percent growth in their net worth from the year before.

By all measures, the superrich are getting even richer in this painful economic climate. We bailed them out, and they used our money to profit even more and pay themselves record bonuses.

And in the middle, on Main Street, people like my brother

Bill are struggling, stuck, scared, and underwater in more ways than one. Unemployment hovers near 10 percent overall and much higher in the hardest-hit states and cities. Job insecurity is even higher and very widespread. In August 2010, foreclosures were proceeding at an average rate of more than three thousand per day. The dream of home ownership in America, with the family home as the source of financial security, is disappearing. Pensions and savings have been lost, and the future seems very uncertain for many. Most of all, people are afraid and they are angry.

The political consequences of fear and anger are reaction and retaliation—against whoever happens to be in power. There are two kinds of populism in American history: one is based on hope and the other on fear—we are clearly living with the latter. The easiest targets of angry voters are their elected officials. Nobody actually likes the people who control Wall Street, but it's hard to figure out ways for ordinary citizens to hold them accountable.

Our government has clearly given us good reason to be angry. Agencies that were supposed to be policing companies became partners in profit. Legislation, instead of creating a level playing field for companies to compete, has too often become a game the wealthy and well-connected manipulate for competitive advantage. It seems that more and more elected officials are working for the companies who give them campaign contributions rather than for the citizens who cast their ballots.

So the political solution being proposed by the punishing populism of the angry middle is to throw the current bums out, and to a certain extent, I understand that. But to simply blame the government for all our problems misses the huge scale of our crisis and misses too many opportunities for change. In this book I argue that "market fundamentalism" is what got us into this mess. Our society is made up of checks and balances, yet the market crash showed that our good moral sense and governmental accountability failed to balance the market's excesses.

This book suggests that the market has become God in our personal lives. We rely on the market to do for itself and for us things it was never intended to do. Our moral values have been replaced by market values.

Both Republicans and Democrats have made the mistake of relying on the people, policies, and mind-sets that led to this economic crisis to get us out of it. Politicians have eroded the rules and regulations that hold banks and corporations accountable. They have cut taxes for the richest Americans, maintained our enormous levels of military spending, and rewarded the moneyed special interests that fund the members of Congress. The answer to what ails us isn't found simply in government or business or the civic sector: the answer is found in restoring balance between all three.

Our nation experienced a huge oil spill since this book was first published. BP's decision to set aside safety for profit led to a disaster for the people, the economy, and the ecosystem of the Gulf Coast, and it became one more painful drama for that beleaguered region of the country. I joined an interfaith delegation that visited the Gulf and talked to the people most affected. We reflected on the consequences of our "addiction" to oil and how this might be an "epiphany" or wake-up call for the nation. But the needle didn't move even a fraction of an inch in Washington toward a new energy future, and the efforts to pass even an inadequate climate change bill collapsed in the Senate during the spill. Since the exploded well was capped (after the worst spill in history), BP has spent $93 million in public relations money to convince us all of how responsible and caring the company really is.

On a recent trip I took from New York to Washington, my Amtrak train was so delayed that I didn't get home until 2:30

a.m. Some "signals" failed just north of Baltimore, and the train had to crawl along for mile after mile at about five miles per hour. On the train, I was reading a *New York Times* column by Thomas Friedman, who had just returned from China, where, he reported to my alarm, the national infrastructure, including its rail system, is significantly superior to our own. I looked around my coach car and pondered how little the trains and tracks had changed in the decades that I have been making this trip.

Have we learned nothing at all? Gratefully, I can say there is another side to this story. Perhaps the power centers of society in both Washington and New York don't control as much as they think, and may be unable to prevent changes under way in the hearts of many on Main Street, and even in some hearts in business and in business schools across the country—where I have been talking to many. And some of that change is also happening in the hearts of American religious congregations whose values are very different from those of the casino economy.

Since the first edition of this book was published, many leaders from the business community have come by just to talk, in a way that my staff describes as being like "Nicodemus at night" (a reference to the Gospel story of a Jewish establishment leader coming, under cover of darkness, to privately talk to Jesus about religion and values). Many speak of the things they fear they have "lost"—values from their faith, the era when bedtime stories passed from parents to children were a nightly occurrence, even early motivations for going into business to make the world a better place and not just to make a profit. Many have critiqued their own behavior, and that of their colleagues, as well as the entire Wall Street culture, with words like *greedy, risky,* and *selfish.* These critics want to redeem the purpose of business, which they believe should be more than just a quarterly profit-and-loss statement. They say too many of their colleagues have confused means and ends and that the market is meant to be the *means* of solving problems and not an *end* in, and of, itself. And most believe that there should be multiple *stakeholders* in business, including workers, customers, the community, the environment, and even future generations. They also believe that the criteria of success should not be determined only by a narrow group of *shareholders*.

Rediscovering Values was prompted in part by my experience of speaking to and with business executives at the World Economic Forum, which convenes an international meeting in Davos, Switzerland, each year. During this financial crisis, the critical question of values has infiltrated the plenary and workshop sessions at Davos, and now there is a Global Agenda Council on Values to help inform the work of the WEF. Davos has convened a new project, the Moral Economy Dialogue, to map where and how the values conversation is changing both discussion and behavior in the business world, and he has asked John De-Gioia, president of Georgetown University, and me to chair the dialogue. What the values of a post-crisis world should be is now a legitimate topic at Davos.

> I CHALLENGED BUSINESS EXECUTIVES TO ENGAGE EACH OTHER ON HOW TO REPLACE THE ETHIC OF ENDLESS CONSUMPTION WITH THE ETHIC OF SUSTAINABILITY.

Some of my most hopeful experiences have stemmed from my speaking engagements at business schools like the Drucker School of Management at Claremont Graduate University and the Wharton School of the University of Pennsylvania. At Wharton's summer leadership seminar, I challenged the assembled business executives to engage one another on how to replace the ethic of endless consumption with the ethic of sustainability. The nodding heads around the room suggested to me that while they might not have the solution, the business leaders present thought it was a fair and important challenge.

I have also been very encouraged by the response to this economic crisis in the faith community. Because local congregations have had to face unemployment and housing foreclosures as real pastoral issues, new solutions are being explored—like some of the ones described in this book. The Great Recession provides members of the religious community the opportunity to reconnect both to their own faith tradition and to their communities and parishes. It is our opportunity to lead by example. I see growing evidence of both our reconnections and our leadership.

I have spoken to churches about what a specifically "Christian" response to this economic crisis could be, to synagogues about how to think about economics in a "Jewish" way, and to Muslim leaders and groups about the implications of Sharia law and Islam for economic behavior. Small business owners who are also lay leaders in their congregations have reported to me about how they and their pastors have helped develop adult Sunday curricula on economics. I have been pleased to hear how many small groups are using *Rediscovering Values* for study and action.

Because of that, we have developed a substantial study guide to accompany this paperback edition of the book as an appendix, hoping that many congregations and groups will commit to serious and sustained study and reflection about what we must learn from the Great Recession and how we can be changed by it.

Families are changing their economic behavior, either out of necessity or by choice, or both. I hear reports of less eating out and more family time together over meals. I see much more scrutiny about consumer decisions and even family discussions with children about those decisions. Both service and giving have become a greater focus for many congregations and families—recalling the fact presented in this book that the Great Depression was, ironically, an era that set the record for charitable contributions in American history. And a new generation of young believers has decided that their economic style of life is an essential element of their discipleship. What it means to follow Jesus has been one of the biggest questions to emerge with new strength, directly as a result of the Great Recession. Young people are asking what "God's Economy" looks like.

Imagine if our national leadership, from many sectors, had said something like this at the beginning of this crisis:

> We are in a terrible economic crisis, brought on by risky, greedy, selfish, and irresponsible behavior and short-sightedness on Wall Street; but none of us are blameless in an economy built on too much consumption and too much debt. The truth is that we have neglected the foundational infrastructure of our nation, physically and morally, over many decades—even before this current financial crisis. So because crisis is both a time of danger and opportunity, we must use this moment as the chance to rebuild our nation's most basic foundations—from our roads and bridges, transportation systems, our entire energy grid, all the way to our moral foundations in our family life, our educational systems, our community service, and solidarity. This must now be our mission in order to make a safer and more renewable future possible. It won't be easy, and it won't happen quickly. But together, with shared purpose and some shared sacrifice, we can rebuild America. It's time to put aside the

> A NEW GENERATION OF YOUNG BELIEVERS HAS DECIDED THAT THEIR ECONOMIC STYLE OF LIFE IS AN ESSENTIAL ELEMENT OF THEIR DISCIPLESHIP.

partisan battles and commit ourselves to a common task that needs all our efforts.

But that leadership has not been offered. A crisis that could have produced a genuinely moral discourse and rare nonpartisan solutions has instead produced an ideological food fight. Business has not self-corrected, but only continued to follow old and failed patterns. Ideological politics have literally sabotaged bipartisan cooperation. Keeping or winning back power has dominated the creative, innovative, and bold visions and solutions we desperately need in order to move forward. We are in a political mess now, and the country is in deep trouble.

So, once again, leadership will have to come more from the bottom than from the top. Congregations and communities will likely be the focus of new thinking, new choices, and new solutions. Those will be based on moral, spiritual, and even theological arguments more than political ones. They will be based upon the understanding that there will be no real long-term economic recovery without a moral recovery. My hope is that this paperback edition of *Rediscovering Values* can help generate discussion in every community that will move us toward that moral recovery, and that each of us can be a part of an economic *conversion* that will save our country—and maybe our national soul.

PART ONE

WHAT
WERE WE
THINKING?

1

SUNDAY SCHOOL
WITH JON STEWART

Crisis is a good time to clarify the meaning of many things—including our economics, our values, and our religion. When crisis hits, it bring us to the place where we begin to question some of our most basic assumptions. It is exactly when the world seems most confusing and events seem most inexplicable that we are forced to go deeper, find past mistakes, and begin to build anew. As I said earlier, if you are asking the wrong question, it doesn't matter how good the answer is, you aren't going to get where you want to go.

The good news is that we are beginning to get some clarity, as more fundamental questions are being asked . . . but they're being asked in unlikely places. You may have missed it—there was an event, a happening, a shift that points to the way out of this crisis. Some likened it to the storming of the Bastille, the Boston Tea Party, or a populist uprising. Some spoke of King Lear's dark fool, who spoke truth when all others were mute; others likened it to a prophet in the wilderness; others finally breathed a sigh of relief as they heard plainly spoken . . . "The king has no clothes."

I call it Sunday School with Jon Stewart. It was early March in 2009, and millions of Americans went to Sunday school, or more accurately, Sunday school came to them through Comedy Central. In the culmination of a weeklong "cable network feud," comedian Jon Stewart invited CNBC's *Mad Money* host Jim Cramer to come onto the *Daily Show,* and what followed sounded like a mix between a confession and a good ol' values lesson.

Stewart asked Cramer about two markets in which we are all participating:

> . . . one that has been sold to us as long term. Put your money in 401(k)s. Put your money in pensions, and just leave it there. Don't worry about it. It's all doing fine. Then, there's this other market, this real market that is occurring in the back room. Where giant piles of money are going in and out and people are trading them and it's transactional and it's fast. But it's dangerous, it's ethically dubious, and it hurts that long-term market. So what it feels like to us—and I'm talking purely as a layman—it feels like we are capitalizing your adventure by our pension and our hard-earned money. And that it is a game that you know is going on. But you go on television as a financial network and pretend it isn't happening.

And the comedian wasn't being funny, he was angry.

> I understand that you want to make finance entertaining, but it's not a f——ing game. When I watch that, I get, I can't tell you how angry it makes me, because it says to me, you all know. You all know what's going on. You can draw a straight line from those shenanigans to the stuff

that was being pulled at Bear and at AIG and all this derivative market stuff that is this weird Wall Street side bet.

Then a moral-values dialogue ensued:

STEWART: But honest or not, in what world is a 35-to-1 leverage position sane?

CRAMER: The world that made you 30 percent year after year after year beginning from 1999 to 2007 and it became—

STEWART: But isn't that part of the problem? Selling this idea that you don't have to do anything. Anytime you sell people the idea that, sit back and you'll get 10 to 20 percent on your money, don't you always know that that's going to be a lie? When are we going to realize in this country that our wealth is work. That we're workers and by selling this idea that of, "Hey man, I'll teach you how to be rich." How is that any different than an infomercial? [1]

Isn't that the problem? The American dream has been turned into an illusion. One distorted almost beyond recognition. And now the illusion has evaporated, the house of cards has fallen, the tide has gone out, and it is high time we seek to understand what happened and what went wrong. Our country has been through severe downturns before, not the least of which was the Great Depression. It was a time of great fear and suffering, but also of redemption and transformation.

Franklin Roosevelt saw the challenges of his day and met them by saying this in his first inaugural address, sounding like a preacher expounding a biblical text:

Practices of the unscrupulous money changers stand indicted in the court of public opinion, rejected by the hearts and minds of men. They only know the rules of a generation of self-seekers. They have no vision, and when there is no vision the people perish. Yes, the money changers have fled from their high seats in the temple of our civilization. We may now restore that temple to the ancient truths. The measure of that restoration lies in the extent to which we apply social values more noble than mere monetary profit.[2]

Comedian Jon Stewart and President Franklin Delano Roosevelt both recognized that a country in crisis needs to confront the illusions that led it astray and return to the values that can form a firmer foundation. The words of both men function as a commentary on a story at the beginning of the ministry of Jesus.

THE MONEY CHANGERS

The Passover of the Jews was near, and Jesus went up to Jerusalem. In the temple he found people selling cattle, sheep, and doves, and the money changers seated at their tables. Making a whip of cords, he drove all of them out of the temple, both the sheep and the cattle. He also poured out the coins of the money changers and overturned their tables. He told those who were selling the doves, "Take these things out of here! Stop making my Father's house a marketplace!" His disciples remembered that it was written, "Zeal for your house will consume me."[3]

A few points about context. This passage is often misunderstood. Jesus' indignation and anger were not fueled by the buying and selling of goods in the temple. In other words, this passage is not an indictment against church bake sales, and I'm pretty sure even a gift shop in a cathedral is still okay! The passage is about greed, not commerce.

The story is set during the time of Passover, when pilgrims

traveling from distant countries came to worship at the temple in Jerusalem. When they arrived, they were supposed to offer sacrifices, but it would have been impossible for these travelers to bring livestock with them on their long journeys. The merchants and money changers conveniently set up shop in the temple's outer court to provide these pilgrims with the scripturally mandated animal sacrifices. However, the worshippers were frequently cheated in this marketplace. Greedy money changers inflated the currency rate (only a certain type of coin could be used in the temple), and the merchants had a monopoly on the sacrifice market.

COMEDIAN JON STEWART AND PRESIDENT FRANKLIN DELANO ROOSEVELT BOTH RECOGNIZED THAT A COUNTRY IN CRISIS NEEDS TO CONFRONT THE ILLUSIONS THAT LED IT ASTRAY AND RETURN TO THE VALUES THAT CAN FORM A FIRMER FOUNDATION.

Interestingly, in his turning over of tables, Jesus specifically targeted the merchants who were selling doves. Doves were the least expensive sacrifice permitted to be offered in the temple and, therefore, were often bought by the poorest of the pilgrims.

It was a marketplace that took advantage of the poor, who had little other choice. It was a "subprime" marketplace in which a few accumulated great wealth for themselves at the expense of those who could least afford to pay. The money changers had taken a place reserved for the values of God, and used it to put their profits first. No doubt these money changers would have argued that they were only responding to a demand of the market, but Jesus didn't seem to see it that way. What was happening in the marketplace was a spiritual and moral problem, not just an economic one.

So do Christians have a responsibility to turn over the tables of an unjust market? Furthermore, as the body of Christ, which is a new temple, do we need to provide an economic witness in the marketplace that reflects God's values of compassion, fairness, and justice?

On Comedy Central, Jon Stewart overturned some tables in his interview with Jim Cramer by asking questions nobody else was asking—at least not on television. How did we move from wealth resulting from real work to wealth coming from the "game" of the casino gamblers of Wall Street? he asked. And why have the media messengers been covering for them? How did the manic metrics of the daily market competition make us forget that real people's lives were at stake? I imagine that maybe the look on the face of the market's chief manic man was similar to the one on the faces of those temple money changers.

> DO CHRISTIANS HAVE A RESPONSIBILITY TO TURN OVER THE TABLES OF AN UNJUST MARKET?

The challenge for our country today is not only to overturn the tables of the money changers, but also to rebuild on the values we have lost. If all we do is flip over a few tables and fail to replace them with what should be there, we can be sure that tables will be uprighted and business as usual will begin again in no time.

TABLES TO BE OVERTURNED

Jesus is a fascinating character. It is easy to envision him as a wise teacher, an empathetic leader who welcomed children, a suffering servant who quietly bore ridicule and injustice. Certainly, he was all of those things. But in the story of Jesus' overturning the tables in the temple, we see something different.

We see a man enraged at injustice and passionately confronting those who exploit the poor. We also learn that there are some things that we all should get angry about, that there are situations where the only appropriate response is confrontation.

Stewart's interview with Cramer struck a chord for me and many other Americans because he touched on some of the things that should make us angry. The leadership of FDR was strengthened when people who were beaten down saw that their leader shared their anger at the injustice of it all. While there are many varied and complex things that went on to lead us to our present situation, I believe there are three primary things that deserve our anger—our righteous indignation.

> THERE ARE SOME THINGS THAT WE ALL SHOULD GET ANGRY ABOUT.

First, we were sold a lie. We were sold an illusion that promised the American Dream was as close as our next purchase. That we could pursue our selfish interests without thought to the consequences, because the "invisible hand" would work it all out in the end. We were told that we did not need to work for wealth, that it would come if only we put our money in the hands of the right stock broker, mutual fund, or stock. Advertisements convinced us that it was all about our own satisfaction and that personal fulfillment was about getting our incomes up and keeping our consumption constant.

Second, the rules of the game failed. It was supposed to be simple. Work hard, get ahead, buy a home, and tuck some money away for the future in a 401(k). If you followed those rules, everything would work in your favor. But good jobs have disappeared, wages have been garnished, and 401(k) savings have disappeared. The rules of the game seem to have worked for those who set the rules, but not for those who played by them.

Third, our good was supposed to trickle down. We were promised that as the rich got richer, the rest of the country would prosper as well. If we handed our finances and ultimately our lives over to those who knew the market the best, it would benefit us all. If we took the virtues of the market and made them the virtues of our lives, we, too, would experience boundless prosperity. Fulfillment would come if we could just trust the market enough to work for us.

This book is full of stories, from people both ordinary and powerful, who used to believe the false promises of easy wealth, used to trust the rules of the game, and used to believe in a "trickle down ethic." But their thinking and living is being transformed, and that is the hope for all of us.

THREE MORAL LESSONS

These failures are reasons to be angry. They are tables worth flipping. They are issues worth confronting. But the ministry and work of Jesus make it clear that anger alone is never sufficient. We need to begin to answer the question of what they should be replaced with. Here is a start:

> THESE FAILURES ARE REASONS TO BE ANGRY. BUT ANGER ALONE IS NEVER SUFFICIENT.

First, relationships matter. The relationship between employer and employee has collapsed from one of mutual benefit to whatever you can get away with. It wasn't that long ago that people knew their bankers and bankers knew the communities they were in. Those relationships collapsed completely with the rise of mortgage-backed securities that made it virtually impossible to figure out who was tied to whom and how. Bank of America got its start as Bank of Italy, giving loans to low-income Italian immigrants whom other banks deemed too risky. The tight-knit nature of the communities in which they loaned and the personal relationships of their "branch" banking positioned them as one of the world's largest banks. But where are they, and we, now?

Second, "social sins" also matter. The excess and opulence of the 1920s that preceded the Great Depression were not seen again until the excess and opulence that immediately preceded our current Great Recession. This is not a coincidence. When wealth comes to those who fail to add value to our economy, that social sin will soon find the sinners out. When we create a cultural habit of spending money we don't have for things we don't need, a disaster isn't far away. And history shows that an increasing gap between the rich and the poor is a prime indicator of imminent collapse.

Third, our own good is indeed tied up in the common good. When the only business concern is the bottom line, then business quickly becomes a race to the bottom. When we recognize that *the common good is our own good* and that civil society, business, and government must work in concert and not in competition, then we

> CARING FOR THE POOR IS NOT JUST A MORAL DUTY BUT PART OF THE COMMON GOOD.

can create business that is not only just, but sustainable. Some have accused Jesus of sounding like he was igniting class warfare by his call for us to care for "the least of these." In our present context, I hope we can learn that caring for the poor is not just a moral duty but part of our own enlightened self-interest. Almost half of the world's population, three billion people, lives on less than two dollars a day—virtually outside of the global economy. Maybe this crisis will help us decide it's time to bring them in.

WHAT THE POPE THINKS

Of course, markets are not inherently bad and can be an effective mechanism for economic growth, which can help to lift people out of poverty. But markets must be tempered by values and judged by fairness. In a recent encyclical, Pope Benedict XVI wrote about the recession and the economy. In writing about profit, he addressed the dangers of idolatry and writes that while profit is useful, once it "becomes the exclusive goal, if it is produced by improper means and without the common good as its ultimate end, it risks destroying wealth and creating poverty." The current economic crisis, he writes, "obliges us to re-plan our journey, to set ourselves new rules and to discover new forms of commitment. . . . The crisis thus becomes an opportunity for discernment, in which to shape a new vision for the future."

He writes about the "pernicious effects of sin" in a market where there is a "speculative *use of financial resources* that yields to the temptation of seeking only short-term profit." This, he says, does not make "a real contribution to local society by helping to bring about a robust productive and social system, an essential factor for stable development." Financiers, he continues, "must rediscover the genuinely ethical foundation of their activity, so as not to abuse the sophisticated instruments which can serve to betray the interests of savers."[4]

> JUST BECAUSE WE CAN AFFORD SOMETHING, DOESN'T MEAN WE SHOULD BUY IT.

The goal is not to destroy the market but to understand its proper place. It is not to get rid of commerce but to build it upon a foundation of values. Just because a bank can extend credit doesn't mean that it always should. Just because consumers can receive credit doesn't mean they should always use it. And just because we can afford something, doesn't mean we should buy it. We need to have a conversation about the difference between wants and needs, between could and should, and to do that, we need to reset some priorities.

2

WHEN THE MARKET
BECAME GOD

In the Great Recession, there are both villains and vices. And both are parts of how we got here. We have been calling good evil and evil good, and we become more and more confused about the differences between the two. The cultural messages over the last several decades have clearly been: *greed is good; it's all about me;* and *I want it all, and I want it now.* Such messages have consequences. The popular messages also told us that if we did not ruthlessly follow these maxims, it was a sign of weakness and deficiency or that we were being stupid not to look out for "number one." If we did not want it all, there must be something wrong with us. The tables overturned in the temple represented not just an economic injustice but a loss of values, and the Great Recession is about more than subprime mortgages; it is the result of a moral crisis.

The story of how we got here is not one of just a few bad apples at the top, a Wall Street conspiracy, or merely some bad public policy. It is, plain and simple, a story as old as humanity:

it is a story of idolatry. We have replaced God with the "invisible hand" of the market, substituted "market value" for "moral values" and attributed all that was good and right to the power of the market to make it so. The market has trumped all else and replaced much of the moral space of society, even questioning the value of having "moral space" where the market does not reach.

THE MARKET HAS REPLACED THE PRACTICE OF CITIZENSHIP WITH THE RITUALS OF CONSUMPTION.

Too often, the market has become like an invasive species, devouring everything in its path; this is what idols often do. It has replaced the practice of citizenship with the rituals of consumption; and the identity of the consumer has replaced the identity of the citizen—even in the strategy of political campaigns, which are now just one more marketing blitz to sell a candidate.

THE GOLDEN CALF

The market has become our "golden calf," our idol of ultimate allegiance. The Technicolor image of a furious-looking Charlton Heston as he played Moses in Cecil B. DeMille's classic production of *The Ten Commandments* is familiar to many of us. The story, found in the book of Exodus, relates that after God led the Israelites out of enslavement in Egypt, they came to Mount Sinai, which Moses climbed and where he stayed "for a long time." While he was gone, the people got nervous that he had disappeared, and they asked Aaron, Moses' brother, to make gods for them. Aaron took the people's gold and fashioned a calf for them to worship; when they saw it, they cried out, "O Israel, these are the gods who brought you out of the land of Egypt!"[1]

This is when God—and then Moses—got angry. Why? Just because they built a golden calf? No. The calf could have been just a work of art, a statue to enjoy. What made the calf an idol was that the people gave the newly created calf the credit for leading them out of Egypt. They gave to the golden calf credit and attributes that belong only to God.

Idolatry comes in a lot of different forms. Today, it is much more subtle than bowing down to a golden calf. It often takes the form of choosing the wrong priorities, trusting in the wrong things, and putting our confidence where it does not belong.

Today, instead of statues, we have hedge funds, mortgage-backed securities, 401(k)s, and mutual funds. We place blind faith in the hope that the stock indexes will just keep rising and real estate prices keep climbing. Market mechanisms were supposed to distribute risk so well that those who were reckless would never see the consequences of their actions. Trust, security, and hope in the future were all as close to us as the nearest financial planner's office. Life and the world around us could all be explained with just the right market lens. These idols were supposed to make us happy and secure and provide for all our needs. Those who manage them became the leaders to whom we looked, not just for financial leadership, but direction for our entire lives. That is idolatry.

Rich and poor alike were sucked into making heroes out of those who seemed to be able to turn everything they touched into gold. Holocaust survivor and Nobel Peace Prize recipient Elie Wiesel lost virtually all of his personal wealth and his foundation's, up to $37 million, to Bernie Madoff's Ponzi scheme. "We gave him everything, we thought he was God, we trusted everything in his hands."[2]

THE MARKET AS IDOL

Most of this did not happen as a result of conscious choices. It happened because we weren't paying enough attention. That is why all of this bears some "religious" reflection, as the market has become all pervasive—a replacement for religion and even for God. It is the market now that has all the godlike qualities—all-knowing, all-present, all-powerful, even eternal—unable to be resisted or even questioned. Performing necessary roles and providing important goods and services are not the same things as commanding ultimate allegiance. Idolatry means that something has taken the place of God. The market can be a good thing and even necessary; but it now commands too much, claims ultimate significance, controls too much space in our lives, and has gone far beyond its proper limits.

> WE HAVE ATTRIBUTED ALL THE GODLIKE QUALITIES TO THE MARKET—ALL-KNOWING, ALL-PRESENT, ALL-POWERFUL, EVEN ETERNAL—UNABLE TO BE RESISTED OR EVEN QUESTIONED.

In what became a prophetic essay, published in *The Atlantic* magazine in March 1999, Harvey Cox, of Harvard Divinity School, wrote about what was happening to us, without any moral or theological reflection, in an article titled "The Market as God." Throughout history, Cox notes, there have always been a variety of different types of markets. But, *meaning* or *purpose* for life, society, and all of civilization always came from different centers of society. It has been a slow growth over the past two hundred years, and an accelerated growth over the past thirty years, that has elevated "The Market" to a godlike status with godlike qualities.

Cox suggests that the market has become *all-powerful* (omnipotent), with the ability to "convert creation into commodities." Natural beauty that used to have value because of the awe it inspires has suddenly been reduced to having value only when chopped up into lots, stuck with a price tag, and dubbed "real estate." The market "*knows all*" (omniscience), and therefore directs our thoughts. It, and it alone, knows what we need, what we want, how much we should pay for it, and how much we should get paid for selling it to others. "Finally," Cox continues, "there is the divinity's will to be omnipresent (all present). . . . The latest trend in economic theory is the attempt to apply market calculations to areas that once appeared to be exempt, such as dating, family life, marital relations, and child-rearing. . . . The Market is not only around us but inside us, informing our senses and our feelings. There seems to be nowhere left to flee from its untiring quest. Like the Hound of Heaven, it pursues us home from the mall and into the nursery and the bedroom."[3]

The market even has its priests, pastors, rabbis, imams, and shamans. These commentators translate the often confusing signals of the Dow, international currency exchange rates, or futures indexes and tell their people what they mean and how they should act as a result. Sometimes they preach famine and the retribution of the market for the sins of the people, and other times they praise the market and the feast it provides. Those who question the market "god" are called heretics and lunatics and are burned at the stake on conservative talk radio.

> THOSE WHO QUESTION THE MARKET "GOD" ARE CALLED HERETICS AND LUNATICS AND ARE BURNED AT THE STAKE ON CONSERVATIVE TALK RADIO.

THE GOOD, THE BAD, AND THE UGLY

Markets are the best ways that humans know how to create goods and services, although they often fall short in fairly distributing them. They structure efficient exchanges that are able to produce mutually beneficial outcomes for the parties involved. Markets are the reason we are able to walk into a grocery store and get the food we need, go to a retail store to buy clothes to wear, and talk with a Realtor to find the homes we live in.

When markets work well, they alleviate poverty and increase well-being. Jeffrey Sachs estimates that before 1800 perhaps 85 percent of the world's population lived in what we today would call extreme poverty. By the middle of the last century, that percentage had decreased to 50 percent; in 1992 it was 25 percent.[4] Today, the official World Bank definition of extreme poverty is subsisting on less than one dollar per day. In 2007, there were one billion people in that category, 15 percent of the world's population. While there are other factors also at work, some of the credit for that does go to the growth of market economies around the world. No one wants to go back to the economic circumstances of two hundred years ago, but that does not mean we should refrain from asking tough questions about our present situation and what this crisis could teach us.

Since the start of the Great Recession, people across the country have been doing exactly that and are starting to learn that idolatry always has consequences. In the story of the golden calf, Moses returned from the mountain, burned the calf, and ground it into powder.

Daniel Gross, author of *Dumb Money: How Our Greatest Financial Minds Bankrupted the Nation*, describes the "Holy Trinity": "low interest rates, deregulated markets, and the ability of financial innovation to insulate markets and the millions of people who depended on them from calamities." But market religion has clearly failed us. Gross points out that to try and blame any one person or group would be a mistake. Instead, he says,

> All of us—investors, home owners, borrowers, lenders, journalists, elected officials, economists, regulators, credit rating agencies—helped assemble this multi-trillion-

dollar "crap sandwich," as House minority leader John Boehner memorably dubbed the situation. . . . The real scandal is that law-abiding, respectable citizens who were operating well within the confines of laws and regulations racked up the overwhelming majority of losses suffered.[5]

IDOLATRY HAS CONSEQUENCES

The results of the economic crisis are record housing foreclosures, empty houses and apartments, plummeting education and retirement funds, lost financial futures, and perhaps most painful, the loss of jobs. The landscape of America is changing because of the Great Recession. Among the changes: cities that have never seen such things before are dealing with a rise of shantytowns filled with the poor and newly poor, reminiscent of the Hoovervilles of the Great Depression, named after the president under whose watch the depression occurred. New York, Los Angeles, and my hometown of Detroit were already accustomed to such encampments of the poorest; but for middle-size towns like Fresno, Seattle, Nashville, and St. Petersburg, seeing people living in tents, lean-tos, and make-do shelters made from scrap material is a new and alarming development. Day labor and minimum-wage work kept many people just on the edge of the economy. But without that work, more and more are falling off the edge.

We now see an alarming and tragic picture in many cities and rural areas across the nation, of the newly poor swelling the lines at food banks, church pantries, and soup kitchens. In addition to those already poor in America (officially 39.8 million in 2008—the highest since 1960—and likely many more in 2009), the ranks of the hungry and even the homeless are being swelled by "the next layer of people," according to Rosemary Gilmartin, who runs the Interfaith Food Pantry in Morristown, New Jersey.

She and others who feed the hungry now speak not only of the lowest rung of previously low-income workers, but also of child-care workers, nurse's aides, service employees, landscapers, housekeepers, secretaries, and, of course, real-estate agents.

Even in upscale places like Lake Forest, Illinois; Greenwich, Connecticut; and Marin County, California, there have been tremendous increases in the demand for donated food since the recession began. Even employees in the banking, computer, and marketing industries are losing jobs, resulting in longer hours for food banks and soup kitchens. Dave Cort, the executive director of a Bay Area food bank, says, "Here we are in big, fancy Marin County, but we have people who are standing in line with their eyes wide open, thinking, 'Oh my God, I can't believe I'm here.'"

Kathleen DiChiara, executive director of the Community FoodBank of New Jersey, sounds the same: "If one of our richest counties has people signing up for food stamps who have never signed up before, that indicates the depth of this problem with the lack of food. . . . It's the canary in the coal mine."[6] We will look at this in chapter 7.

Food banks were already reporting increased demand with the domestic poverty rate rising each year of the Bush administration; homeless shelters were reporting a shift in their residents from mostly single men, often with addiction problems, to families with children—many of whom had somebody working but not making enough to afford adequate housing. The recession has, of course, made all that worse, with many more people falling into poverty, as unemployment has continued to rise. Many of the newly poor are utterly lost and unsure how to navigate their new situation. "These are people who never really had to ask for help before," says Brenda Beavers, of the Salvation Army in New Jersey. "They were once givers, and now they're having to ask for assistance." The veteran provider of social services reports,

"They look shell-shocked. . . . I've had people walk back out and say, 'I can't do this.' "[7]

We really shouldn't be surprised by all this. Austrian econo-mist Joseph Schumpeter, writing in 1946, warned against what has now come to pass in the Great Re-cession: "Capitalism creates a critical frame of mind which, after having de-stroyed the moral authority of so many other institutions, in the end turns against its own."[8] Schumpeter did not argue to replace capitalism with some other system, but rather that capitalism must be checked and find its foundation in moral values.

> MANY OF THE NEWLY POOR ARE UTTERLY LOST AND UNSURE HOW TO NAVIGATE THEIR NEW SITUATION.

When you so divorce morality from economy, the moral health of the society is the first causality; then we all begin to worry about where all the values have gone.

Adam Smith, the father of modern economics and the origi-nator of the idea of an "invisible hand," agrees as well. In a fa-mous passage, Smith argued: "It is not from the benevolence of the butcher, the brewer, or the baker, that we expect our dinner, but from their regard to their own interest. We address ourselves, not to their humanity but to their self-love, and never talk to them of our own necessities but of their advantages."[9]

This is often true. When we go to the grocery store today, our primary thought is not about being generous to the person stocking the shelves or the clerk who scans our groceries, but to getting the food we need for our family. The employee stocking the shelves and the clerk scanning the food are there because they receive a paycheck that comes from the money we just handed over for food. We all benefit.

To leave it at that, however, is to miss something crucial and to ignore a large portion of Smith's work. Before he wrote his famous economic treatise, *The Wealth of Nations,* Smith wrote another volume, *The Theory of Moral Sentiments.* In it he wrote, "To feel much for others and little for ourselves . . . that is the perfection of human nature." Is this a contradiction? No. It's a question of which comes first. Our moral system, our beliefs about what is right and good, must always come before our economic system. Our moral system must provide the foundation for and encompass our economic system, and when it happens the other way around, we see, as Schumpeter would say, that our economic system can destroy our society and then itself. When economics comes before values, we have idolatry.

CHALLENGING THE IDOL

Should the market be all-powerful, all-knowing, and all-present? Is there anything that money can't buy—or shouldn't? It's a rhetorical question that is now critical to ask. Michael Sandel is a professor at Harvard whose course on "Justice" has become the most popular on campus—drawing over a thousand students into a Socratic dialogue on the big moral questions of our time. Sandel says, "We need a public debate about the moral limits of markets." Limits? We have not wanted to talk about limits, but that may be one of the principle reasons we are now in such trouble. The Wall Street collapse, corporate excesses, and bad behavior by CEOs must lead to new social regulation of the markets—after decades of deregulation that allowed the market to creep into more and more of our lives and have now led to economic crisis. And that will be a battle with corporate America and the financial giants, who are already shamelessly fighting any reforms of their behavior. But are new

> IS THERE ANYTHING THAT MONEY CAN'T BUY—OR SHOULDN'T?

scattershot regulations enough? Perhaps we need to ask some deeper questions, like the place, role, and limits of the market itself.

Do we want the market and market values to prevail everywhere and in all things? Are there some areas of life where market values should not determine what is most important—personal and family relationships, ethics and religion, community and public service, and social justice? Should every good become a commodity? How far should the market reach? Should everything be privatized, or should we keep some space for the common good? Sandel says that the economic crisis marks the end of the last three decades of "market triumphalism." He suggests that the idea that markets are the primary instruments for achieving the common good are now "in doubt."

Where should the market govern, and where should other values—personal, social, and ethical—hold sway? Should monetary norms crowd out more intrinsic norms in every area of life? Are, in fact, certain things degraded when market norms are allowed to be the ultimate measure? Are there certain social values and practices that are higher than market values? Markets do leave their mark. And when market incentives are allowed to replace all other incentives, there will always be social consequences.

The provision of personal goods and services is a good role for the market. But do we really want the market to control all our public services as well? Do we want the profit motive to define the way we run our hospitals, prisons, and all our social services? I'm glad I can bring my boys to a privately owned and operated amusement park so that they can ride roller coasters, but I'm not so sure I would want a private corporation or individual to own Yellowstone National Park. And should the market be allowed to intrude into the most intimate and personal areas of our lives, such as relationships, the family, childbirth, medical choices, the whole frontier of genetics, and the inner life of religion and spirituality? Ultimately, and perhaps most important, do we want the ethics and values we see in modern advertising to shape the spirituality of our children?

If the market ultimately defines what gets our attention, we will be defined by the moral limits of the marketplace. For example, if I were getting my primary information about the global health crisis from the advertising messages of the market, I might think the greatest threats to humanity today are not malaria and HIV/AIDS but rather a massive epidemic of erectile dysfunction! And what gets our attention is one of the surest marks of the moral health of any society.

> DO WE WANT THE ETHICS AND VALUES WE SEE IN MODERN ADVERTISING TO SHAPE THE SPIRITUALITY OF OUR CHILDREN?

Given all that has now been revealed from the Great Recession and its results, it is worth remembering Harvey Cox's prophetic warnings. He wrote, "At the apex of any theological system, of course, is its doctrine of God." And as this theologian began his discipline of reading the business pages of the newspapers each day, he noticed similar "dialectics" that he had often pondered in his extensive readings of historical theology and church history. His theological conclusion was that while there have always been markets of one sort or another, they were never thought to be gods; but that "The Market," shrouded in mystery and awe, has now risen to the status of "First Cause." Former restraints on the market disappeared as it indeed took on more godlike qualities, "whose reign must now be universally accepted and who allows for no rivals."

In claiming the power to define what is real and true, and bowing to no limits beyond itself, the market now claims "a comprehensive wisdom that in the past only the gods have known." And like a god to be feared and worshipped, we now can even know the market's moods on a daily basis. "The Market is 'apprehensive,' 'relieved,' 'nervous,' or even at times 'jubilant.' . . . Like one of the devouring gods of old, the market—aptly embodied in a bull or a bear—must be fed and kept happy under all circumstances."[10] And to even question the market's "high priests" and their declarations is to commit heresy. The worship of this false god, The Market, has become quite ecumenical. Across denominational and faith persuasions, herds of us are bowing down to the doctrines and dictates of The Market.

But this crisis presents us with an opportunity, not just to be smarter and more prudent about our economic lives, but to change something much deeper—to reject the idolatry of our market worship, to expose the idols that have ensnared us, and to reduce "The Market" to simply "the market," asking the market to again serve us, rather than the other way around.

Indeed, it could be that the religions of the world might help lead the way here, challenging the idols of the market and reminding us who is God and who is not—a traditional and necessary role for religion. "The earth is the LORD's and the fullness thereof, the world, and they that dwell therein,"[11] say both Christianity and Judaism: it does not belong to the market. Let us also remember that human beings are merely stewards of God's creation; not its masters. And we humans are the ones who preside over the market—not the other way around.

And despite our differences, the *religion* of the market has become a more formidable rival to every religion than we are to one another. But together now, we could challenge the dominion of the market, by again restoring the rightful worship of God. The market's false promise of its limitless infinity must be replaced with the acknowledgment of our human finitude, with more humility and with moral limits—which are essential to restoring our true humanity. The market's fear of scarcity must

> THE DICTUMS
> OF GOD'S
> ECONOMY SAY
> THERE *IS*
> ENOUGH, IF
> WE *SHARE* IT.

be replaced with the abundance of a loving God. And the first commandment of The Market, "There is never enough," must be replaced by the dictums of God's economy; namely, there *is* enough, if we *share* it.

The crisis of the Great Recession could do more than prompt a reset of our economic life; it could restore a sense of right worship.

PART TWO

HOW WE GOT HERE

3

GREED IS GOOD

Our cultural sins have now found us out. And while *wealth* does not seem to trickle down from the top of this economy to the bottom, it does seem that *bad behavior* and *bad values* do trickle down, and all of us have some serious self-reflection to do. The new maxims, "Greed is good," "It's all about me," and "I want it now" have replaced old virtues. Being number one is now more important than anything or anyone else and has become even more important than *the One* who points us to things beyond ourselves—*the One* who will ultimately hold us all accountable. A market based on greed and fear has tugged on some of the worst things in us, and we are now paying the consequences.

We live in a popular culture where celebrities have replaced real heroes, and our celebrities now include CEOs who make as much or more than the actors and the athletes. We are in no short supply of stories of millionaires and billionaires who seem to have no other passion or motivation in life than to accumulate wealth, possessions, and "toys" as quickly and as much as they can. Enough is never enough in a culture of greed.

For example, on February 17, 2009, over a dozen federal agents raided the offices of Sir Mark Allen Stanford in investigation of a \$9 billion Ponzi scheme. In June he was arrested and charged with defrauding investors. The press quickly dubbed "Sir" Mark as the "mini-Madoff." He had a fleet of private planes worth over \$100 million. He lived in a castle in Florida complete with a moat and a man-made cliff that was demolished in 2008, reportedly to build something even bigger.

But also disturbing is not just the values of the villains in our current economic story, but that so many of us wanted to be like them. Our society has promoted the cultural sin of covetousness, which offers either enormous opulence or the experience of vicarious wealth through watching the opulent on television.

> ENOUGH IS NEVER ENOUGH IN A CULTURE OF GREED.

We have created an industry of voyeurism, with reality TV shows holding up the wrong kind of heroes and teaching us to strive to be just like them. We know that something has gone wrong when Donald Trump, on the TV reality show *The Apprentice,* is offered as a cultural role model for a new generation of business leaders.

AIG bonuses and bankrupt CEOs' private jets demonstrate that a sense of entitlement is not just an attitude we can blanketly attribute to the poor, but is a real problem of many rich people, who believe they are entitled to be treated like kings and queens of old, whether or not they are successful.

Because of our fascination with wealth, our economy has been sustained by buying things we don't need, with money that we don't have. Who we admire is a test of the integrity of a society.

WALL STREET

While the adulation of greed has pervaded much of our lives, nowhere was it said quite so clearly as in the movie *Wall Street*. In an unforgettable monologue by Wall Street tycoon Gordon Gekko, the heart of the acquisitive economy is simply laid out. At a stockholder meeting in the midst of a "hostile takeover" of the fictional company Teldar Paper, Gekko told those assembled: "Greed, for lack of a better word, is good. Greed is right. Greed works. Greed clarifies, cuts through, and captures the essence of the evolutionary spirit. Greed in all its forms, greed for life, money, love, knowledge has marked the upward surge of mankind, and greed will not only save Teldar Paper but that other malfunctioning corporation called the USA."

> WE TURN ALL OF LIFE, LOVE, KNOWLEDGE, AND RELATIONSHIPS INTO COMMODITIES AND LET THE MARKET GIVE THEM A PRICE TO SEE IF THEY THRIVE OR GO BANKRUPT.

For Gordon Gekko, to an extreme, and for most of us, to a certain extent, this view of the world has been true. Our economy and, Gekko argues, our entire country, should find its motivation in greed. It is greed that will separate the wheat from the chaff, the strong from the weak, those who are successful from those who will be eliminated. We turn all of life, love, knowledge, and relationships into commodities and let the market give them a price to see if they thrive or go bankrupt.

YACHT CULTURE

In his book *Richistan: A Journey Through the American Wealth Boom and the Lives of the New Rich*, Robert Frank describes an international superrich society that now dominates the global economy. He calls the supereconomy Richistan, and its inhabitants Richistanis. In a particularly shocking investigation, we see the parable of greed played out in a description of the superrich yacht culture.[1]

Frank begins the account of one yacht owner: "Don Weston used to feel special cruising the world in his 100-foot yacht." But soon, a 100-foot yacht wasn't impressive anymore, as neighboring yachts reached 130 feet, then 197 feet, and beyond. One of those large boats owned by Larry Ellison is called the *Rising Sun*, described as a "floating palace that tops 450 feet and has more than 80 rooms on five stories. Along with the usual gyms and swimming pools, *Rising Sun* has a twin-hulled landing craft to carry a four-wheel-drive Jeep ashore." The result for Don and his yacht? " 'I used to think I had a good-sized boat,' Mr. Weston sighed. 'Now it's like a dinghy compared to these others.' It's safe to assume that at no other time in American history has a 100-foot boat been referred to as a 'dinghy.' "

What is the mentality, morality, psychology, or spirituality of having such extravagant wealth? When Ellison took his first holiday on the boat in early 2005, he told friends it was too big—that he and his wife felt like they were the sole patrons in a giant restaurant. "Well, I do think it's excessive," Ellison said. "It is absolutely excessive. No question about it. But it's amazing what you can get used to." Frank also points to the personal reflections of Paul Allen, who "uses his six-story *Octopus* as a main boat, but keeps his 300-foot *Tatoosh* and 198-foot *Meduse* on hand as backups and guest yachts for friends and family."

It is a game that has no end. As soon as a yacht becomes the world's biggest, another Richistani starts to build one even larger. The largest yacht in the world today is owned by Saudi royals and comes in at 482 feet, but it will soon be overcome by one being built for Sheikh Mohammed bin Rashid al Maktoum, ruler of Dubai, whose yacht, when finished, will measure 525 feet. But even that won't last for long; a secretive Russian oil tycoon is building another yacht to beat it and refuses to release the length to make sure that no one can get a head start in beating his record.[2]

> THIS IS AS SOCIALLY UNBELIEVABLE AS IT IS MORALLY UNCONSCIONABLE IN A WORLD WHERE HALF THE GLOBAL POPULATION STILL LIVES IN POVERTY.

This is as socially unbelievable as it is morally unconscionable in a world where half the global population still lives in poverty. Robert Frank then goes through the same amazing litany of "big-dog cars" worth hundreds of thousands of dollars, planes for hundreds of millions with alligator-skin toilet-seat covers and houses with tens and even hundreds of thousands of square feet, including four-hundred-square-foot walk-in closets with conveyer-belt systems (like at a dry cleaners), which bring your clothes to you quickly and easily.

NORMAL-PEOPLE GREED

Most of us cannot imagine the sort of greed that would make a one-hundred-foot yacht feel inadequate; most of us have never even seriously considered owning one, but this same vice is played out in our lives every day and lies at the root of the Great Recession.

Time and time again my wife and I receive mailings or telephone calls asking us, almost begging us, to take out another mortgage on our house. There was always a sound of incredulity and disbelief that we would not want to take "full advantage of all our equity," so that we could buy the "essentials" we just must have. Another property maybe, a second car—or at least a bigger, fancier one than we have now—a flatscreen for every room, and a new wardrobe for every season.

An August 2008 story in the *New York Times*[3] walked through some of the history of banks marketing "second mortgages," or home equity loans. The challenge the banks were facing was that second mortgages had always been a last resort for people in tough economic times, and they wanted to expand their use. It quotes Pei-Yuan Chia, a former vice chairman at Citicorp: "Calling it a 'second mortgage,' that's like hocking your house. But call it 'equity access,' and it sounds more innocent."

The ad campaign Citi started in 2001 was "Live Richly." In 2003 it included an ad that, according to the article, said "a home could be 'the ticket' to whatever 'your heart desires.' " In 2004, Banco Popular said in its "Make Dreams Happen" ads: "Need Cash? Use Your Home." A 2006 PNC Bank ad pictured a wheelbarrow as the "easiest way to haul money out of your house." Wells Fargo in 2007 simply stated, "Seize your someday."

Quoting a Harvard economist, the article went on to say, "It's very difficult for one advertiser to come to you and change your perspective. But as it becomes socially acceptable for everyone to accumulate debt, everyone does." And that's the key: what has been deliberately and carefully made "socially acceptable" was, not too long ago, thought to be irresponsible—both financially and morally.

> "AS IT BECOMES SOCIALLY ACCEPTABLE FOR EVERYONE TO ACCUMULATE DEBT, EVERYONE DOES."

The struggle to distinguish between what we actually need and what we simply want can be a challenge for anyone. If you add in the estimated three thousand advertisements we are exposed to every day and the increasing consumption of all those around us, that challenge gets even more difficult.

Does it bother anyone else, besides me, that virtually everything now has a "sponsor"? You can't hear the score of a ballgame without hearing it from the Bud Light scoreboard; and my old Tiger Stadium in Detroit was replaced by a new ballpark named after a bank.

Our children learn these attitudes early in life. One study found a 66 percent increase from 1976 to 2006 in the number of high-school students who said that "having lots of money" was "extremely important."[4] One of my kids approached us and suggested he might like to have an iPhone. The simple fact that I was quite certain that this expensive piece of technology would be lost or cracked within a week ruled out an iPhone for my elementary-school child. But I was intrigued as to how this had suddenly become a desire for my son. The reason? A classmate had just gotten one.

CONSPICUOUS CONSUMPTION

Robert Frank didn't just describe the wealthy; he also provided some diagnosis. He recalls the classic 1899 treatise on wealth, *The Theory of the Leisure Class*, in which author Thorstein Veblen coined the phrase "conspicuous consumption" to explain the excesses of the Gilded Age. When a group of people or a society are no longer working for subsistence to feed, clothe, and provide basic shelter, they look for ways to identify their own wealth, status, and class: "Veblen said that the wealthy bought expensive goods as a way to identify themselves as members of the nonworking leisure class. Waste and excess weren't just tolerated by the rich; they were necessary to show rank on the social scale."[5]

While Thorstein Veblen and Robert Frank concerned themselves primarily with the very wealthy, it is easy to see how true this has become for most Americans, those who can afford and those who can't. Consumption has become an important source of our identities in America.

Without a clear sense of self, a strong identity, and a community of purpose, it seems our default mode is to identify ourselves by the things we own. We try to convince ourselves and signal to others who we are almost solely by the clothes we wear, the cars we drive, the restaurants we eat at, and the houses we own. An identity built on these things is a weak one indeed; and it's an identity that can easily dissolve, crack apart, or be taken away from us.

> CONSUMPTION HAS BECOME AN IMPORTANT SOURCE OF OUR IDENTITIES IN AMERICA.

Jesus put it like this, "Don't store up treasures here on earth, where moths eat them and rust destroys them, and where thieves break in and steal. Store your treasures in heaven, where moths and rust cannot destroy, and thieves do not break in and steal. Wherever your treasure is, there the desires of your heart will also be." [6] Notice Jesus doesn't say, "where your heart is, there will your treasure be," affirming the popular defense today that goes something like this: "While I may have wealth, it isn't that important to me; it's what is in my heart that is important." Well, Jesus says the reverse is true: where your treasure is, that's where your heart is also most likely to be.

If I teach my son at a young age that he should base his identity, his popularity, and his friendships on having the coolest cell phone of any of his friends, he'll discover that those relational things all disappear with the cell phone. If, instead, his identity is rooted in something deeper, if it is rooted in values that do not disappear with a cell phone or a stock portfolio, then it is secure.

In *Wall Street,* Gordon Gekko's young protégé, Bud Fox, came to question the principles by which his teacher and mentor was living:

GORDON GEKKO: It's all about bucks, kid. The rest is just conversation.

BUD FOX: When does it all end? How many yachts can you waterski behind? How much is enough?

GORDON GEKKO: It's not a question of enough, pal. It's a zero-sum game. Somebody wins, somebody loses.

But it turns out that greed isn't so good after all. Greed is, indeed, a vice and not a virtue; and it takes the market's focus on self-interest way too far. Self-interest without the restraint of ethics has done us in during the Great Recession. As I write today, in September 2009, President Obama travels to speak on Wall Street and tell the leaders of the nation's financial markets that they have to show more "responsibility" in their behavior. Such a sermon on economics would have been laughable just a short time ago, but one hopes the president gets *some* "Amens" to that message today. Unfortunately, his words seem to have fallen on deaf ears, as top banking executives continue to receive huge bonuses while opposing all efforts at regulatory reform.

> SELF-INTEREST WITHOUT THE RESTRAINT OF ETHICS HAS DONE US IN DURING THE GREAT RECESSION.

Perhaps even worse is what unbridled greed has done to our values, and we all worry about the impact of valueless economic ethics on the moral formation of our children. In the end, we really don't want our kids to operate with the unrestrained ethics of greed. At the most basic level, and despite all of our own behavior over several years now, we know that greed isn't good for us and certainly isn't good for our children.

In *Wall Street*, the classic dialogue between Gordon Gekko (played by Michael Douglas) and Bud Fox (played by Charlie Sheen) isn't the last word. There is also the discussion between

Bud and his working-class father (played by Martin Sheen, the real-life father of Charlie), who isn't impressed by the flashy but empty ethics of Gekko and clearly doesn't like what is happening to his son. Bud's father tries to counter the ethics of greed.

Carl Fox, the dad, gives his son some very good advice—which sounds quite prophetic now in light of what has happened to all of us in the Great Repression: "Stop going for the easy buck and start producing something with your life. Create, instead of living off the buying and selling of others."

Perhaps the best counter to the culture of "greed is good" is an admonition that comes from the heart of our moral and religious traditions that remind us that "enough is enough." We'll explore this concept in depth in a later chapter.

4

IT'S ALL ABOUT ME

America's strong and admirable tradition of individual liberty and responsibility has been replaced by a culture of narcissism. The value of the individual is central to American history, but extreme individualism teaches that life is all about me and not about "them"; about besting and beating our neighbors, rather than loving or even looking out for our neighbors. It teaches that people basically get what they deserve, and if you start helping those around you, you may be destroying the natural order of a social competition. And it's more than a little ironic how so many religious fundamentalists who reject scientific evolution seem to so heartily embrace a new social Darwinism—the survival of the fittest.

Advertisers confirm that *it's all about me* and tell us that the next new product, purchase, outfit, vacation, car, or home will finally make us happy. But it doesn't. It only sets the stage for the next false consumer hope and great subsequent letdown. Community has been replaced by isolated individuals locked in an endless and stressful match to have the biggest house, the largest televisions, the sexiest bodies, the most exotic vacations, and even the most successful children (have you heard about "Harvard track" preschools?).

THE SHOCK OF GREENSPAN

"Those of us who have looked to the self-interest of lending institutions to protect shareholder's equity (myself especially) are in a state of shocked disbelief,"[1] then Federal Reserve chairman Alan Greenspan told a congressional committee on October 23, 2008. Self-interest was supposed to keep us safe from harm. Greenspan had argued year after year that many of the dangerous and risky financial instruments that became part of the collapse should not be regulated. The reasoning was that the bankers who were using these instruments were the ones who knew them best and that they would make rational decisions based upon their own interest. If something was too risky, they wouldn't do it because it might hurt them too much. You did not need government to step in and stop them from doing things that might be harmful in the long run. If only people thought enough about themselves, the market would be "self-regulated."

After Greenspan's testimony, the chairman of the committee, Representative Henry Waxman, said to the man known as the

> SELF-INTEREST WAS SUPPOSED TO KEEP US SAFE FROM HARM.

Maestro, "You found that your view of the world, your ideology, was not right, it was not working." Greenspan responded, "Precisely. That's precisely the reason I was shocked, because I had been going for forty years or more with very considerable evidence that it was working exceptionally well."[2]

The former chairman of the Fed is right. Self-interest often does do its job, but not always. Basic self-interest can turn into self-obsession, narcissism, and dangerous pride. The inward focus can make it so that we stop thinking about how our actions might hurt others or even how we might hurt ourselves a year or two down the road.

James Grant, editor of *Grant's Interest Rate Observer,* was quoted in the *Washington Post* after the hearing, saying that Greenspan had trusted that "markets and societies move on belief systems. The belief system of finance featured the notion that someone with unusual power to see around corners and through walls and into the future was running things, and that someone was Alan Greenspan."[3]

PRIDE BEFORE THE FALL

"Pride goeth before a . . . fall," is quite possibly the most famous Bible verse in popular use in the King's English. It comes from Proverbs 16:18 in the King James Version of the Bible that says, "Pride goeth before destruction, and a haughty spirit before a fall." This is not because the Almighty is out to get a laugh from the failures of those who have gotten too big for their britches. It is rather because pride puts us in situations where failure is imminent. It was what led so many bankers and hedge fund managers to take risks that they never should have. It was pride—the belief that they understood the world better than they did, that they could read markets like a map, and that they could manage age risk without worry—that put them in such a dangerous position. The clear lesson is that protecting against pride is a good way to protect yourself. Hubris was often considered the greatest sin of the ancient Greek world. Hubris was considered an excessive pride, often seen when the protagonist of a story would

> PRIDE PUTS US IN SITUATIONS WHERE FAILURE IS IMMINENT.

challenge the gods or overreach in battle. If hubris took over, the protagonist's end was near.

The Greeks tell a story of another kind of pride that is familiar to us today. Narcissus was known as a handsome young man, but vain. He met his fate when he became entranced by the image of his own reflection and eventually killed himself because he was tormented by unrequited love. The Great Recession is not just a story of a few prideful bankers; it's also the story of another kind of pride that has seeped throughout our culture: narcissism. It is not an understatement that in the years leading up to our economic fall, we had the exact same mentality. The numbers bear it out.

Jean Twenge, PhD, and W. Keith Campbell, PhD, in their book *The Narcissism Epidemic: Living in the Age of Entitlement,* examined data from thirty-seven thousand college students and found that since the 1980s, narcissistic personality traits rose just as fast as obesity. By 2006, one in four college students showed above average narcissistic personality traits—agreeing with the majority of questions on a standard measure of narcissistic traits, a 30 percent increase from the early 1980s. Two-thirds of the respondents on the 2006 test scored above the mean score in a 1970–1985 sample of the same test.

Narcissism is beyond a healthy self-esteem just like hubris is far beyond a basic understanding of self-interest. As a father, I believe it is important to say to my children: "Believe in yourself" and "You are special." I do believe in my two boys and think they are special, and it's not narcissism for them to know it. What is narcissistic and what is harming our culture is when children or adults believe they are the exception. The problems come when "I am special" turns into "I am an

> THE PROBLEMS COME WHEN "I AM SPECIAL" TURNS INTO "I AM AN EXCEPTION."

exception." When "I believe in myself" becomes "I do not believe in others."

The story of the Garden of Eden tells us that pride was the original sin. The serpent came to Adam and Eve and told them that if only they listened to him, they would "be like God." It doesn't take much to stoke the flames of our vanity, and billions of dollars in advertising revenues are spent every year to do it. Promoting "conspicuous consumption," as mentioned in the previous chapter, advertisers tell us that if we buy their products, everyone will know how special we are, how smart we are, how beautiful we are, and how rich we are. One jewelry advertisement encouraged the expensive accessories because "you can't wear your corner office out at night."

In 2005, Ameriquest made waves in the competitive field of Super Bowl commercials by portraying themselves as an "open minded lender." Their ads showed an innocent person getting caught in the midst of what looked like a quite embarrassing situation. Viewers laughed at the husband innocently cooking dinner for his wife, when spilled tomato sauce covers their cat in red and the knife he was using to chop onions looks like a murder weapon. But these entertaining commercials from a now defunct lender sent a clear message: It doesn't matter what you have done in the past, there won't be consequences, and you deserve this loan. Larger properties, second homes, days at the spa, expensive sports tickets were all sold with this message. What used to be privileges became entitlements.

Started in 2004, the social networking site Facebook now has more than 200 million active users. If Facebook were a country, it would be the fourth largest country in the world right after the United States and ahead of Indonesia.[4] Technology has allowed for the creation and sharing of new information at levels never seen before in human history. But, it has also created an unprecedented number of ways to say "Look at me!" In fact, this desire has prompted the growth of one of the entertainment industry's fastest growing sectors, which I mentioned briefly: reality television.

REALITY TELEVISION

Maybe you can remember back to 1973 and the controversy around the airing of *An American Family*, a twelve-part PBS documentary that was an early precursor to today's reality television. It was considered quite controversial as the film crew followed the beginnings of a difficult divorce. From the *Lifestyles of the Rich and Famous* to MTV's *Real World*, our country has become obsessed with watching and mimicking the "reality" portrayed on television.

In 2006, the International Cinematographers Guild announced that the filming of reality television had jumped 53 percent in just one year, accounting for 40 percent of all on-location TV production and employing thirty thousand people.[5] This type of unscripted television now accounts for one-quarter of all primetime broadcasting and is the sole daytime content of many more cable channels.

It makes business sense for the networks—popular shows like *American Idol* can command up to $1 million for a single thirty-second advertising spot, and these shows often cost less than half of regular programming to produce. The creators of these shows are, of course, responding to a very clear demand of the market. People watch them. They talk about them. They discuss the lives and actions of the figures they see playing out in these TV dramas time and time again. When the show is over, these new celebrities make the rounds of the talk shows, and the biographies and autobiographies soon start appearing on bookstore shelves.

Paparazzi photos are now a multimillion-dollar industry. In

the mid-1990s there were only an estimated twenty paparazzi working in Los Angeles.[6] Today there are an estimated one-hundred fifty, plus hordes of "citizen paparazzi" who sell their photos to online dealers, who then sell them to other publications. A photo of Brad Pitt and Angelina Jolie with their new baby in June 2006 went for $4.1 million, and pictures of Ashton Kutcher and Demi Moore's wedding in 2005 went for a reported $3 million.[7]

These prices are all supported by "the market." There is a demand for them; people make money off of them. But just because a market demand exists doesn't mean it's a good thing. It doesn't mean it's right. We need to ask ourselves how this is affecting our lives and how it is affecting our decision making. How many times have we seen a celebrity in a new car and, as a result, wanted one ourselves? How many times have our kids seen another child on television and wanted the toy she was playing with? How many times have we fallen into unhealthy habits or lost self-worth by observing those portrayed in the celebrity photos or on TV shows? How many times have we modeled our own behavior after what we've seen acted out on reality television or justified behavior because at least it's not as bad as what was reported in the most recent celebrity tabloid?

We might not call our celebrities heroes, but they become role models by default, by the amount of time we spend watching their lives and allowing ourselves to be influenced by them. We have all too often become passive receptors of Hollywood-manufactured lives and behaviors without fundamentally questioning them. All of this feeds into the all-about-me mentality.

This isn't meant to sound simplistic, but it really is quite simple. The

> WE MIGHT NOT CALL OUR CELEBRITIES HEROES, BUT THEY BECOME ROLE MODELS BY DEFAULT.

stories that we hear, the stories that our kids hear, really do matter. When we hear stories about persons who overcame huge obstacles to achieve great things or sacrificed everything for a cause greater than themselves, we are inspired to be more like them. But when our stories focus on characters who are only in it for themselves, always want more, and will do anything to get it, we can easily be influenced for the worse.

THE GOOD SAMARITAN

Another familiar Bible story is important to remember today. In response to the question "Who is my neighbor?" Jesus told the story of a man who traveled from Jerusalem to Jericho. Along the way this man was attacked, beaten, stripped, robbed, and left by the side of the road for dead. Both a priest and a Levite came along the road and passed by on the other side, not stopping to help. But then a Samaritan, who was considered a religious outcast at the time, saw the man and stopped to help. The story goes on to say that not only did he stop to help, but he brought the wounded man to an inn to be cared for and paid for his recovery.

This story taps into so much of our basic understanding of what it means to be a good neighbor and a good person. It is easy to imagine yourself in this same story. The right thing to do is so clear that you would, without hesitation, stop and help the injured stranger. The reality is, however, that each of us regularly passes up opportunities to love our neighbors.

Imagine walking down that dangerous road and coming upon that wounded man. As you take in the scene, you realize that the robbers could still be lying in wait for some kind-hearted person just like you to stop, so they could rob him also. Would you still want to stop? Surely, there are other people traveling along the road better equipped to handle that type of medical emergency. How about now? What if you were on your way to a business meeting and being late could cost you a major deal and the paycheck your family is counting on. Would you still stop?

Researchers at Princeton University in 1970 decided to test a group of seminary students in a good Samaritan scenario with a few complications thrown in to see how they would react.

These seminary students were told they were participating in a research experiment regarding seminary students and their vocations. After being interviewed, the students were told they needed to give a talk in another building on campus—some were told to speak on the parable of the Good Samaritan and others on vocations for seminary students. The researcher would give them directions to the building, telling some of the students that they had a few minutes before it began and telling others they were already running late.

On the way to give their talks, each student would encounter an actor playing a distressed person clearly in need of help. The true test was to see if the students stopped to help or even noticed the person in distress. While it might seem intuitive that the students who were thinking pious thoughts about the importance of helping others might be more likely to stop and help a stranger in distress, the researchers found no such thing. It failed to change behavior at all. When they analyzed personality profiles and subjective measures of "religiosity," these, too, failed to predict whether or not the student would stop and help. The one factor that had a significant impact upon behavior was whether or not they were in a hurry.

> THE ONE FACTOR THAT HAD A SIGNIFICANT IMPACT UPON BEHAVIOR WAS WHETHER OR NOT THEY WERE IN A HURRY.

From this experiment the authors offered several insights. "It is difficult not to conclude from this that the frequently cited explanation that ethics becomes a luxury as the speed of our daily lives increases is at least an accurate description." Still others, they thought, did not seem to ignore ethics but, "instead, because of the time pressures, they did not perceive the scene in the alley as an occasion for an ethical decision." They were simply moving too fast to even notice that an opportunity to help a neighbor in need was right in front of them.

Still others, the researchers noted, seemed to be in the midst of a conflict. They were hurrying along exactly because they were already helping out the researchers and did not want to fall through on their obligations to them by stopping to help someone else. "And this is often true of people in a hurry; they hurry because somebody depends on their being somewhere. Conflict, rather than callousness, can explain their failure to stop." [8]

Being a good neighbor to a person in immediate distress sometimes means that a commitment to be somewhere else at a certain time has to slide. Choices like these are often where we experience the crux of neighborliness and reach beyond our own self-interest.

A BETTER YOU

I ran across a website promoting "Mommy Makeovers," noting the rise in plastic surgery for recent mothers who wanted to get back to their prebaby body state. The article states, "Motherhood has its rewards . . . sagging or shrunken breasts and protruding stomachs are *not* among them." The regular package includes breast augmentation, breast lift surgery, and tummy tucks.

In 2006 more than 325,000 tummy tuck, breast augmentation, and breast lift surgeries were performed on women between the ages of twenty and thirty-nine, according to the American

Society of Plastic Surgeons.[9] It's not just for mommies either, but their children as well. In 2005 over 330,000 procedures were performed for young people under the age of eighteen.[10] From 2006 to 2007 the number of teens getting breast augmentation jumped 55 percent.[11]

Narcissism has made a huge business of plastic surgery. What was once focused on trying to correct the effects of burns, accidents, or other medical trauma has become the surgical way to become a "better you."

SOCIAL CREATURES

Our American tradition of the protection of individual rights and liberty is essential to who we are as a culture and nation. But the strength of our relationships and the depth of our communities is the other side of that value—one that we have now forgotten. We are an interdependent people, in need of relationships, in ways we are just beginning to understand. Our dependence upon strong communities and ties to others is essential to our identities and even the maintenance of our own humanity. After an in-depth study of prisoners held in isolation, *New Yorker* writer Atul Gawande wrote, "Human beings are social creatures. We are social, not just in the trivial sense that we like company, and not just in the obvious sense that we each depend on others. We are social in a more elemental way: simply to exist as a normal human being requires interaction with other people."[12]

A now famous, or infamous, study by Henry Harlow in the 1950s involved raising baby rhesus monkeys in isolation from one another and their biological mothers. The effects were disturbing. The monkeys would grow up stronger, larger, and healthier than other monkeys more normally socialized or raised in the wild, but as they grew, they would exhibit more and more disturbed behavior—pacing in their cages, rocking, staring blankly, and even self-mutilation.

Another study introduced socially isolated monkeys into a monkey community later in their lives. The results were a type of social shell shock. One in six were dead within five days after refusing to eat, and the rest never did normally socially integrate.

Just one week of solitary confinement for humans begins to slow brain wave activities. One in three prisoners held in solitary confinement develops acute psychosis with hallucinations. Senator John McCain, who suffered under horrendous torture, referred to solitary confinement as one of the worst types of treatment he ever received while a POW. Terry Anderson, a journalist who was kept prisoner by Hezbollah for seven years, after experiencing extended periods of isolation had this to say, "I would rather have had the worst companion than no companion at all." [13]

The antidotes to narcissism and extreme individualism are, again, some very old moral and spiritual values: *humility* and *community*.

If there was a "high priest" of the economy in recent years, it was certainly Alan Greenspan. Earlier in this chapter, we looked at the unraveling of the self-interest principle he so strongly advocated. Greenspan seemed to be a wizard, smarter than the rest of us mortals, essential to the well-working of the financial system, and almost indispensable to political leaders of both parties—none of whom seemed to have the courage to even consider replacing him with any other wizard to run the Fed. What a heretical thought!

But it turns out that Greenspan was more like the Wizard of Oz, standing behind a curtain and projecting his larger-than-life persona and ideas on a big screen for all to watch with fear and awe. And when Dorothy's little dog, Toto, pulled the curtain back with the Great Recession, the little Wizard didn't seem so all-knowing or powerful. After being so exposed, the proper response is humility, which is the quality the very human Wizard of Oz demonstrated.

To his credit, Alan Greenspan has also shown contrition as the projections on his big screen have shown themselves to be illusions.

Greenspan said:

> So the problem here is something which looked to be a very solid edifice, and, indeed, a critical pillar to market competition and free markets, did break down. And I think that, as I said, shocked me. I still do not fully understand why it happened and, obviously, to the extent that I figure out where it happened and why, I will change my views. If the facts change, I will change.

And that's the key, a willingness to change our views and our values. "It's all about me" hasn't worked so well—for our economy, for our families, and for our souls. But some good old-fashioned humility can offer us the chance to rediscover an older and better idea, again rooted in our best moral traditions: *we're in this together.*

5

I WANT IT NOW

Immediate gratification has clouded our sense of the future—mine, yours, ours, our children's, and the planet's. In our credit-card culture, we can have everything we want the moment we want it—never mind the enormous debt we are accumulating. My Depression-era parents wouldn't have thought to buy things before they had the money to pay for them; but my children are being raised in a culture where plastic is money, cash is free at ATMs, and what we want is what we need. There was a time when people bought things only when they had the resources for it, but we have clearly forgotten the difference between what we need and what we want. We need to have that flatscreen, high-definition television right now, and for that, we are willing to sacrifice the future.

Cheap money, the ethic of buy now, pay later and living on lines of credit has taught us to expect what we want, when we want it. We have strung ourselves out on caffeine and Black-Berrys so that everything can and, indeed, must be now, now, now. I have an agnostic friend who was curious about the virtual

> RICH AND POOR ALIKE HAVE FALLEN INTO BAD SPENDING PRIORITIES, WASTING THEIR INCOMES ON SHALLOW AND UNNECESSARY CONSUMER PURCHASES.

religious experience that's now available through all of the new technology. He once asked me, "Will it give you more time to pray?"

Rich and poor alike have fallen into bad values and bad spending priorities, too often wasting their incomes on shallow and unnecessary consumer purchases. I know veteran poverty activists who conduct "faith and finance" or "financial literacy" workshops for the poor, to teach better spending priorities and practices. It's time we all took the workshop.

ENDLESS CHOICES AND POSSIBILITIES

I'll admit it, I have a weakness for Starbucks grande skinny lattes, with no-fat milk, a Splenda, and a dash of mocha powder on top. That drink is only one of the 87,000 different drink combinations that Starbucks serves today. Long gone are the days when I would have to be home on a specific night and time to watch a particular TV program, a presidential debate, or a game. We can now all just TiVo the world, or just get it online, or on YouTube. A laptop and wireless internet connection can connect us instantly with tens of thousands of movies, huge libraries, and archives of music.

We are used to not only getting what we want when we want it, but having what we want customized for us at our time and place of choosing. I enjoy being able to get a cup of coffee that I like and knowing that I don't need to rush home right at eight o'clock to catch my favorite show. But, with all of these changes to the world around us, do we ever stop and ask how they are changing us?

Comedian Louis C.K., in an interview with Conan O'Brien about the economic crisis, noted that it might be a good thing if we could go back to the Stone Age for a while. Why? "Because everything is amazing and nobody is happy."

> WITH ALL OF THESE CHANGES TO THE WORLD AROUND US, DO WE EVER STOP AND ASK HOW THEY ARE CHANGING US?

He described how different things were when he was growing up: "If you wanted money you actually had to go in the bank for the three hours it was open back then . . . and then when you ran out of money you would just say, 'well I guess I can't do any more things now.'" It is quite telling when the idea of only spending money when you have it is the punch line to a joke.

When Louis C.K. sees young people complaining that their phones are going too slow or won't send a message right away, he says, "Give it a second! It's going to space! Can't you just give it one second to get back from space? Is the speed of light too slow for you?"

He described his first flight with one of the new technological amenities now available on some airplanes—wireless internet. When the flight attendant got on the intercom to let the passengers know that the internet was no longer working, the passenger next to him slammed his laptop shut and said, "This is bulls***!" The comic then made what has to be one of the most prophetic comments on our emerging "It's all about me" popular culture: "How quickly the world owes him something he only found out existed ten seconds ago."

DEBT: SERVICE TO MASTER

Debt is supposed to serve us. Students are able to enter college immediately after high school and gain an education that can prepare them to be better citizens, workers, and public servants because of student loans. Through mortgages, young families are able to purchase homes that they would not be otherwise able to purchase for decades. Entrepreneurs are able to start businesses and create jobs because of business loans. Nonprofits are able to start up or grow because of the loans they receive. A family can respond to an unexpected emergency with credit that they can pay back later when they are able to do so. Credit, when used well and wisely, is a very good thing.

But, like lots of good things in our world, debt can turn bad quickly. It can become like a prescription from a doctor to help a patient get through a period of pain that then turns into an addiction. What was intended to be a service has become the master. Debt that was intended to be a response to an emergency can become like an opiate, which gives us an irresistible craving for more. What was meant to be a tool to help us accomplish long-term goals became a long-term master that replaces all goals except that of servicing the debt. Imagine a young student with long-term goals and aspirations who graduates and finds that his or her decisions after college are entirely mandated by the need to pay off debts.

> LIKE LOTS OF GOOD THINGS IN OUR WORLD, DEBT CAN TURN BAD QUICKLY.

In 2006, the United States Census Bureau determined that there were nearly 1.5 billion credit cards in use in the United States. A stack of all those credit cards would reach more than seventy miles into space—or be almost as tall as thirteen Mount Everests. The Census Bureau also reported that there were 159 million credit cardholders in the United States in 2000, which grew to 173 million in 2006, and that number is projected to grow to 181 million Americans by 2010. At the end of 2008, 78 percent of American households—about 91.1 million—had one or more credit cards, and their total credit-card debt reached $972.73 billion.

Nearly half of U.S. families, 46 percent, had credit-card debt, the average per household being $10,679 at the end of 2008. In the last twelve months, 15 percent of American adults, or nearly 34 million people, have been late making a credit-card payment and 8 percent (18 million people) have missed a payment entirely.[1]

Debt has continued to grow across the board. Between 1995 and 2004 our country's richest 1 percent took on $383 billion in debt. Just 5 percent of our population accounts for 20 percent of our entire debt.[2] In the 1980s a disturbing trend began to emerge. Debt is a problem for rich and poor alike. But the fastest growth of debt from credit cards began occurring among those with the lowest incomes.[3]

Credit-card debt is increasingly becoming a problem among college students. The average college senior now has six credit cards and carries a $3,200 balance. Between credit cards and student loans, an increasing number of college students say they are significantly altering their career choices because of large amounts of debt.[4]

MARKET VALUES AND
SOCIAL COST

In 1720, the *Grand-Saint-Antoine,* a merchant ship, was placed under quarantine by officials in the French city of Marseilles. Several crew members had become sick and died from the plague. But this effort to stop the spread of the plague from the ship to the city was soon ended by the city's merchants, who pushed for the authorities to release the ship from quarantine so they could bring its valuable cargo to market.

The disease proceeded to kill fifty thousand people in the city, about half of its population, and an additional fifty thousand in the surrounding area. Those one hundred thousand needless deaths ensued from the cargo's being delivered quickly and efficiently to market.

Since the 1980s there has been a strong push for market deregulation, cutting the funding for regulatory agencies and reducing codes and requirements for business and industry. Federal funding for the Food and Drug Administration was cut 30 percent during the Reagan administration, and over the past thirty-five years, budget cuts have forced a 78 percent reduction in inspections by the agency.[5] Newt Gingrich called the FDA the "number one job killer in America." The inspectors and the agency cost too much money, it was argued. The standards to which they held businesses were too costly for businesses to bear.

It's true. A jar of peanut butter will probably cost more if the plant in which it is manufactured is required to guard vigilantly against contamination or face hefty fines. Children's toys get more expensive when you carefully check to make sure they don't contain lead paint. Is it a price worth paying? In January 2009, eight deaths were linked to peanut butter containing salmonella, and over 575 people were sickened. The Centers for Disease Control estimates that 5,000 people die each year from food poisoning and another 325,000 are hospitalized.[6]

Regulation can, indeed, hurt efficiency; and government agencies, of course, should always be aware of that. But we need to ask ourselves, *Is efficiency always our top concern and driving value?* What social costs are we willing to bear to achieve efficiency? We always want to make sure that life-saving drugs are available as quickly as possible, but the 27,000 who died when safety concerns about Vioxx were covered up should give us pause as to how quickly.

Ultimately, when it came to the spread of the plague in Marseilles, who was to blame? The merchants who lobbied for the release of cargo from the quarantined shipment of course should share some of the blame. But in some ways, they were just doing their job of trying to get their goods to market and make a profit. It was the government regulators who bore the greatest failure. Their job was not primarily profit, but safety. When they let the profit interests of a few override their mandate to look after the safety of many, they failed. While businesses and those who run them should always do their personal best to maintain high standards, we should be upset when government fails to live up to its standards of looking out for public safety.

> WHEN THE GOVERNMENT REGULATORS LET THE PROFIT INTERESTS OF A FEW OVERRIDE THEIR MANDATE TO LOOK AFTER THE SAFETY OF MANY, THEY FAILED.

TEXTING WHILE DRIVING

Communication never seems to take a break. We are almost always in constant contact with one another. Having a cell phone certainly helps my efficiency, and I am not pining for the days of rotary phones, but have we thought much about what this greater efficiency in communication costs us? Text messages first became commercially available in 1992—today the number of text messages sent and received every day exceeds the population of the entire planet.

In June 2008, five female friends from Rochester, New York, died in a collision with a tractor trailer. The driver had been texting moments before the crash. The teens had just graduated from high school the week before.[7] In December 2005, there were 9.8 billion text messages sent. That number has grown to 110.4 billion in December 2008.[8] Over 20 percent of all drivers are sending text messages while driving. If you single out the eighteen-to-twenty-four-year-olds, that number goes up to 66 percent.[9] Texting is just one more layer to our wanting it *now*.

In June 2009, *Car and Driver* performed some experiments to see how texting while driving affected drivers' ability to safely control their vehicles. The results, while not up to full scientific rigor, weren't good. It turns out that drivers' reaction times slowed more significantly than if they were above the legal alcohol limit.[10]

Just because it is possible to text while driving doesn't mean it is a good idea. Just because it may be efficient does not mean it is worth the risks. This is why state governments are now stepping up across the country, banning the practice of texting while driving, and ticketing violators.

THE EARTH GROANS

But the greatest impact, the most damaging consequence of the new maxim "I want it now," is the disaster for the earth itself and, therefore, for future generations. The "ethic of the earth" has to do with the longer time frame of seasons and years, and sustainability. But "I want it now" interrupts all the natural cycles, and it is a violent assault upon the earth—who is indeed our mother.

> "I WANT IT NOW" INTERRUPTS ALL THE NATURAL CYCLES, AND IT IS A VIOLENT ASSAULT UPON THE EARTH— WHO IS INDEED OUR MOTHER.

Our increasing demand for electricity to power the growing number of devices the "I want it now" culture requires is destroying more and more of our earth. According to a recent news report, Americans now have an average of twenty-five electronic products per household. And many of them are power hungry—new flat-panel TV sets use more electricity than refrigerators.[11] Coal-powered electricity-generating plants are still the largest source of our electricity, and as the demand grows, they require more and more coal. Traditional deep mining is very labor intensive and dangerous—we've all been riveted to the news of coal mine collapses with trapped miners. So the easy way out is now what is called "mountaintop removal." Heavily forested mountains are clear-cut of timber, then the top layers are blasted off with dynamite to expose seams of coal that can be mined from the surface. It's cheaper, safer, and more efficient.

But the problem is that it also destroys the land—leaving gaping scars where once stood wooded mountains—and destroys the communities in its vicinity. Waste from the operations is simply dumped into nearby streams, polluting the water and causing frequent flooding. Hundreds of families and communities in Virginia, Kentucky, West Virginia, and Tennessee have been driven off the land by this growing method of mining.[12]

And when the next "must-have" appliance arrives, it requires that we somehow get rid of what we already have. Buying a bigger and better flatscreen television means disposing of the old one. The problem is that each of our older cathode-ray tube televisions includes roughly four pounds of lead. The Environmental Protection Agency (EPA) estimated that in 2007, 26.9 million older televisions were disposed of—20.6 million of them thrown in the trash, while only 6.3 million were recycled. The EPA also estimates that nearly 100 million remain in storage, still fully workable, but unwanted by their owners.[13]

Another growing problem is cell phones. As our cell phones gave way to the next phase—BlackBerrys, and now iPhones, what do we do with the old ones? Again, all too often, they end up in landfills—an estimated 130 million cell phones a year are simply thrown away. Cell phones contain a variety of toxic metals—including cadmium, beryllium, antimony, lead, and arsenic. Those 130 million phones have 65,000 tons of these hazardous materials that are now leaching into our groundwater systems.

According to the EPA, only about 13.6 percent of so-called e-waste was recycled in 2007. And even recycling old electronic devices can pose problems. The Electronics TakeBack Coalition, an organization working to promote green design and responsible recycling in the electronics industry, says "A large portion of the hazardous electronic waste collected for recycling in the U.S. is actually exported to developing countries. There the products are dismantled and separated using such crude and toxic technologies that workers and communities are exposed to many highly toxic chemicals."[14]

Another example is our insatiable desire for beef—whether it's fast-food hamburgers or top-quality steaks. The average American eats a hundred pounds of beef a year. Producing that much beef requires large amounts of pasture to feed the steers, and huge amounts of forest are destroyed to create the open pasture. One of the largest is in Brazil, where since 1970, over 232,000 square miles of Amazon rainforest have been cut down for pasture land—nearly half of that since 2000. And 60 to 70 percent is attributed to cattle ranching, largely producing beef for export.[15] The destruction of this environment leads to the extinction of numerous plants and animals, while the production of beef is estimated to cause 18 percent of the world's greenhouse-gas emissions—more than all forms of transportation combined.[16]

Simplifying our diets would go a long way toward both saving irreplaceable natural resources and slowing the rate of global warming—both growing threats to our future. We don't all have to become vegetarians, but neither do we need to consume the amounts of beef that we now do.

To use a biblical image, it can seem that the whole of creation is "groaning" while it "waits with eager longing" for we children of God to free ourselves from our current lifestyles and desires.[17]

The ethic of "I want it now" clearly doesn't work. In fact, it works against our own balance and well-being, as well as that of our families whose healthy schedules require more space, grace, leisure, and a more human pace of life. And it works against the earth, whose natural ebbs and flows require the gifts of patience, time, rest, and care. Perhaps the best ethic in response to our short-term and destructive maxim is the one that comes from indigenous peoples who say we should evaluate every decision by its impact upon seven generations in the future.

> PERHAPS THE RESPONSE TO OUR SHORT-TERM AND DESTRUCTIVE MAXIM IS TO EVALUATE EVERY DECISION BY ITS IMPACT UPON SEVEN GENERATIONS IN THE FUTURE.

PART THREE

WHAT WE GOT OURSELVES INTO

6

WHEN THE GAPS
GET TOO BIG

For the 2006 Davos World Economic Forum, I was asked to speak on "Should we despair of our disparities?" Facing a room full of CEOs and political leaders, I talked about a subject not too familiar to them—biblical archaeology. I described how the archaeologists exploring ancient Israel discovered a fascinating thing. When they dig into the past, they sometimes find artifacts that suggest a relative economic equality among people—not a sameness, but a relative sharing of prosperity with no great gaps and gulfs. During those periods, it turns out, there were no prophets—no Amos, Isaiah, or Jeremiah. But in other periods, like the eighth century B.C.E., the historical remains show great chasms between the people, huge palaces amid small shacks, etc. And it was during those times that the prophets rose up to rail against the disparities.

Afterward, I kept being asked, "Jim, is that really true? Because if it is, it is quite amazing and explains an awful lot!" While I admitted that preachers sometimes exaggerate to make a point,

I told them these facts of biblical archaeology were indeed true and reveal critical lessons we've forgotten, to our peril.

History teaches us that when the gap grows between the rich and the poor, when the middle gets increasingly squeezed, and those at the bottom are almost completely forgotten, a crash is about to come. The last time that inequality in America was as great as it is today was in the Gilded Age just before the Great Depression. Our religious traditions do indeed point the way: in times of relatively shared prosperity, there are no biblical prophets, because they are not needed. But when inequality is on the rise, the prophets rise up to thunder the judgment and justice of God.

The God of the Bible seems not to mind prosperity—if it is shared. But when it is not, God gets angry. And when wealth becomes more and more concentrated, bad things begin to happen to us: social bonds begin to unravel, societal morale erodes, and resentment sets in when we perceive great unfairness.

For three decades, we have experienced a socially engineered inequality that is really a sin—of biblical proportions. We have indeed seen class warfare, but this war has been waged by the wealthy and their political allies against the poor and the middle class. Does anybody really think that a change in the ratio of CEO salaries to average worker pay from 24-to-1 (1965) to 431-to-1 (2004), is a good thing?[1] In 2008, that has dropped slightly as the recession has hit even corporate executives, but it is still 319 to 1.[2]

> THE GOD OF THE BIBLE SEEMS NOT TO MIND PROSPERITY—IF IT IS SHARED.

The religious teaching of "the preferential option for the poor"—that a commitment to the poor is central to the gospel—has been replaced by deliberate social and political decisions to create a "preferential option for the rich." From tax policy to every little perk of life, the rich just keep getting richer.

This deliberate and carefully calculated redistribution of wealth from the middle and the bottom to the top is perhaps the most important social change in America over the last several decades, but it is one that has gotten very little attention—because the wealthy also have the capacity to effectively control what gets attention. Their own media pundits have even made the R word—"redistribution"—a bad word that no "responsible" person is allowed to say out loud. It would plunge us into "class warfare"! And yet, redistribution is exactly what the most wealthy and their political representatives have accomplished—redistribution to them, with little attention and even less accountability. They're right; it is class warfare. And the upper class has won the battle for the last three decades—at the expense of the poor and middle class and the health and well-being of the economy, and at the cost of some very important social values. The result of all this is a broken social contract and a shattered social covenant that must be reestablished. We should have listened to the prophets.

DAYS OF RELATIVE EQUALITY

The huge economic chasms that now exist are an aberration from much of our own American history. After World War II, our country entered an age of unprecedented wealth, growth, and relative equality. There was no argument about whether the average American was better off from the time the war ended until the 1970s.

This postwar era lasted until the mid-1970s and saw a growth in benefits for average Americans in the work force of 2.5 to 3 percent a year. The median family income doubled between

1947 and 1973. And this growth usually occurred with only one parent working and workers putting in fewer hours, as the workday shortened and five-day work weeks became standard.[3] At the end of World War II, only 30 percent of the population had health insurance, but by 1970 it was above 85 percent.[4] And many workers also came to benefit from standard pensions to ensure a decent standard of living through old age.

This was the country I grew up in. Most parents hoped that their children would grow up better off and have more opportunities than they did growing up. And many did. But these three decades of growing prosperity didn't last. Stagflation set in during the mid-1970s, due in large part to spiraling oil prices caused by OPEC restraints on the production of oil. The resulting economic downturn ushered in the era of "market triumphalism" begun by the new Reaganomics.

Taxes were cut, and markets and industries were deregulated. Government, it was said, was the problem. Get government out of the way, and the miracle of the market will take over. Rich people will spend their money well and invest it wisely, creating more jobs, opportunity, and wealth for everybody. This market ideology and idolatry, which we have already discussed, infused public policy. And now we are seeing the results.

THE CHASM

In 1969, in my hometown of Detroit, Michigan, General Motors was the country's largest corporation, and Charles Johnson was the CEO. It was quite a scandal when his salary was set at what we thought was the astronomical sum of $795,000, or $4.3 million in today's dollars. Even with his average worker making $9,000 a year, or $40,000 in today's dollars, and with excellent health and retirement benefits, Charles Johnson was making eighty-eight times more.[5]

Today, America's largest corporation is Walmart, and its former CEO Lee Scott Jr. made $17.5 million annual salary, 900 times the pay of his average worker.[6] This means that every two weeks Mr. Scott made roughly what an average employee at Walmart would make in a lifetime.[7] Different pay for different work with different degrees of difficulties and responsibilities makes sense to most people. But is anybody really *that much* more valuable or worthy than anybody else?

At first glance, that might seem like a lot of money, but Mr. Scott's $17.5 million in compensation hardly places him very high on the list of well-paid CEOs. *Forbes* reported that, for 2005, Richard Fairbank at Capital One Financial won the prize for compensation by raking in $249.4 million.

> EVERY TWO WEEKS MR. SCOTT MADE ROUGHLY WHAT AN AVERAGE EMPLOYEE AT WALMART WOULD MAKE IN A LIFETIME.

Countrywide Financial, a name now nearly synonymous with subprime mortgages and dishonest lending practices, compensated its CEO quite well before the scheme all fell apart. In 2006 Angelo Mozilo reported $141.98 million in earnings, putting him at number seven on the *Forbes* list.[8] That year, if you wanted to be included in the top 100, you needed to be compensated to the tune of at least $18 million. Steve Jobs topped the list with $646.6 million.[9] Stanley O'Neal, the CEO of Merrill Lynch, who was responsible for pushing his company heavily into mortgage-backed securities, took home a $14 million bonus in 2006 and then walked away in 2007 with a severance package that was worth, at the time, $162 million.[10]

And all that compounds the scandal; these enormous gaps in compensation don't even correlate to success. In fact, they often come after failure. Metrics don't matter, just money. The expectation of entitlement now shapes the demands of the corporate elites—the sense that they deserve the compensation that makes them into our modern royalty.

You might be impressed by these CEOs until you compare them to the hedge-fund managers. The same year Mr. Fairbank made $249.4 million, James Simons of Renaissance Technologies, a hedge fund, reported earning $1.5 billion; T. Boone Pickens was close behind with $1.4 billion.

> THE EXPECTATION OF ENTITLEMENT NOW SHAPES THE DEMANDS OF THE CORPORATE ELITES—THE SENSE THAT THEY DESERVE THE COMPENSATION THAT MAKES THEM INTO OUR MODERN ROYALTY.

The gaps in accumulated wealth are similarly shocking. Mr. Scott's compensation seems paltry when you consider that the family of Walmart's founder, Sam Walton, is estimated to be worth $90 billion. That level of wealth in *just one family* is roughly equivalent to the $95 billion in wealth of the bottom 40 percent of Americans, all 120 million of them.[11] The nation's wealthiest 1 percent have more than doubled their share of national wealth. That top 1 percent now controls over one-third of the nation's wealth, more than the entire bottom 90 percent combined.[12] Is it merely the land of opportunity that allows one family to make more money than 120 million of its fellow citizens, or is it a skewed system and a stacked deck that results in such massive inequality?

THE RISING TIDE LIFTS ONLY THE YACHTS

A rising tide was supposed to lift all boats, but it didn't. It lifted only the yachts of the most wealthy. If you compare wage growth in the post–World War II boom to the growth from the early 1970s until today, only the top 1 percent have done better. The richer you are, the better it gets. The top one-tenth of one percent saw their incomes increase five times over, and the top one-hundredth of one percent are seven times richer than they were in 1973.[13] In 2005, before the current economic collapse, the top 1 percent of households received seventy times as much in average after-tax income as the bottom one-fifth of households, and more than twenty-one times that of the middle one-fifth of households.[14] The peak income year for the bottom 90 percent was 1973, when the average income for that group, adjusted for inflation, was $33,000 a year.

This gap has gotten wider, while, even after you adjust for inflation, the value of the per-hour output of the average worker has risen almost 50 percent since 1973. If these gains in productivity had been evenly shared across the workforce, the typical worker's income would be about 35 percent higher now than it was in the early 1970s.[15] To put it differently, if the typical household had shared evenly in the productivity gains, they would have earned about $20,000 more in 2006 than they actually did.[16] Again, most of those gains went to the top 10 percent of wage earners who experienced far above average wage growth, while the bottom 90 percent experienced below average growth or just lost out.[17] Not to share in the fruits of their own productivity and to see most of the prosperity from it go to their bosses at the top, is not the way to make workers feel they have much stake in the economy.

Remember, none of this "just happened" but was the deliberate result of public policy and political de-

THIS GAP WAS THE DELIBERATE RESULT OF PUBLIC POLICY AND POLITICAL DECISIONS MADE TO BENEFIT ONE GROUP OVER ANOTHER.

cisions made to benefit one group (shall we say "class"?) over another. And much of it has to do with radically changed tax policy.

From 1979 to 2006, the top tax rate on earned income was cut in half, the tax rate on capital gains was cut almost as much, and corporate income tax was reduced by a quarter. These changes have resulted in huge gains for the wealthiest of Americans but not much for anyone else.[18] Taxes in 1979 were already significantly lower than they were during the boom years. Under Republican president Dwight D. Eisenhower, the top tax bracket was at 91 percent; Democratic president John F. Kennedy cut that to 70 percent. No, that is not a typo; I couldn't believe that percentage either when I first heard it. Today it is only 35 percent!

These numbers are stunning. What we always hear is that since the numbers of the superrich are so few, reducing their share of society's wealth wouldn't make much of a difference. But that simply isn't true anymore. The wealth has become so great for those at the top, and their portion of society's resources has grown so much, that the richest getting less of a share *would* indeed make a great difference to the rest of us. There are enormous sums of money now going to the people on the top that cannot be justified, even economically, but certainly not morally and spiritually.

A good friend of mine often says that the enormous growth of American inequality is the gorilla in the room of every political conversation that nobody wants to talk about or even recognize. But again, these levels of inequality always indicate that problems are coming, and coming soon. The last time our country experienced this type of inequality was in the years running right up to the Great Depression. Income inequality has hit two high-water marks in the past hundred years or so, 1928 and then 2007.

BEFORE THE COLLAPSE

In 2007, right before the collapse, the superrich set a new record. For the first time, the top 1 percent made more than a thousand times that of the average family in the bottom 90 percent. A real milestone in the quality of our life together. The year that comes closest to matching that kind of disparity was 1928, right before the market crash that marked the beginning of the Great Depression.[19] In numbers released by the Federal Reserve Board in the summer of 2009[20] we saw that in 2007 the top 1 percent held $3.3 trillion in wealth, or 33.8 percent of the entire nation's wealth. The next 9 percent of the richest Americans held 37.3 percent of the nation's wealth . . . the bottom 90 percent only 28.5 percent. What is even more disturbing is that this analysis left out every person on the *Forbes* Top 400 wealthiest individuals. They held $1.3 trillion in wealth, more than the entire bottom 50 percent in our country.[21] Four hundred people holding more wealth than half of the whole country is a disparity over which we should, indeed, despair and would likely make the disparities of biblical times pale in comparison. Perhaps this Great Recession will provide an opportunity for some modern-day "prophets" to speak out again.

The global gaps are very stark as well. In 1820, in the world's wealthiest region, Great Britain, the average per person income was three times higher than the world's poorest region, sub-Saharan Africa. Today, the world's wealthiest nation is the United States, and the average per-person income is twenty times greater than that of the world's poorest region, still sub-Saharan Africa.

FOUR HUNDRED PEOPLE HOLDING MORE WEALTH THAN HALF OF THE WHOLE COUNTRY IS A DISPARITY OVER WHICH WE SHOULD, INDEED, DESPAIR.

If you make $50,000 a year here in the United States, you are part of an elite class of the world's wealthiest 1 percent. Surprised? Try a quick exercise. Go to www.globalrichlist.com, enter your income, and see how you compare when it comes to the distribution of the world's wealth.

THE GREAT LIE

There is a great lie, a pervasive myth that goes along with such disparity. I consider this lie no less than a biblical heresy that has seeped into our culture and our country. It claims that those who are wealthy are so because they are responsible and righteous, and those who are poor must be irresponsible or even immoral. The rich have done all the right things, and the poor must have done something wrong. It is the belief that great physical riches indicate that God must be pleased with your actions and that poverty suggests God's disfavor and even punishment.

The lesson we must relearn is that rich and poor alike can be villains and heroes. Those with wealth and those without are capable of both great virtue or vicious vice.

King Solomon, one of the wealthiest men in the world during his day, wrote in the book of Ecclesiastes that:

> *The race is not to the swift*
> *or the battle to the strong,*
> *nor does food come to the wise*
> *or wealth to the brilliant*
> *or favor to the learned;*
> *but time and chance happen to them all.*[22]

This is a clear acknowledgment that might does not make right and a wealthy person is not necessarily a good person. Jesus, in his Sermon on the Mount, said that God "causes his sun to rise on the evil and the good, and sends rain on the righteous and the unrighteous." The Great Recession has shown that indeed, when it rains, the rain falls on us all.

We all need to recognize the signs of sickness in our society as a whole, within our families and friends, and even in ourselves. The beliefs that greed is good, it's all about me, and I want it now ended up being not only bad for ourselves, but harmful to those around us and disastrous for our economy.

THE NEW OLD VALUES

But the story must not end there. This is the time to ask the right questions about what type of people we want to be, what the character of our communities should look like, and the kind of country we could become.

It is not enough for us to identify what went wrong—we need to understand what we can do differently so that we don't make the same mistakes over again. I don't think the answers are very far away. Some of the greatest changes we need to make and lessons we need to learn reside in some of our deepest and oldest values—values that we seem to have forgotten or at least failed to make into the priorities they should be. These are the values many of us remember as kids in Sunday school or from children's books read to us by our parents and that we read now to our own sons and daughters.

> SOME OF THE GREATEST CHANGES WE NEED TO MAKE AND LESSONS WE NEED TO LEARN RESIDE IN SOME OF OUR DEEPEST AND OLDEST VALUES.

I like to call these the "New Old Values." It is to these we now turn and hopefully will learn to restore to the back streets, Main Streets, Wall Street, and your street.

7

ON LISTENING
TO CANARIES

One day a young state senator from West Virginia came
to one of our big mobilization gatherings focused on
ending poverty. His father had been a coal miner, and
he told the story of how coal miners used to take canaries down
with them into the mines. I was fascinated to learn why miners
used to take these little birds with them as they descended into
the earth. It was because the canaries' sensitive respiratory systems could easily detect a toxic environment—faster than the
miners' could. And when the canary started to cough and choke,
it was a sure sign that the miners should scramble out of the
mine before they were also in trouble.

Senator John Unger suggested that the canary becomes,
therefore, a metaphor for the poor and vulnerable in any society,
and their well-being is a monitor of societal well-being. When
the poor begin to suffer, it will not be long before the rest of us
will also feel it. We missed those warning signs of this current
economic crisis. Ultimately, the common good is our own good,

> ULTIMATELY, THE COMMON GOOD IS OUR OWN GOOD, AND THE BEST THING FOR ALL OF US IS THE RIGHT THING FOR THE LEAST OF US.

and the best thing for all of us is the right thing for the least of us.

A social covenant has indeed been broken, and an earlier covenant—which my generation grew up assuming would bring us prosperity and relative equality—is completely foreign to a younger generation. When I was growing up, at least the upper-middle class, the middle class, and the lower-middle class all went to the same church and knew they were in this together—both economically and spiritually. That is now a distant memory.

REDISTRIBUTION IS NOT A FOUR-LETTER WORD

If, in the years leading up to this recession, you were only watching the Dow or the NASDAQ, you thought things were going pretty well. If you were watching the incomes of the country's top 1 percent, you thought things were booming. So we could have started talking about the R word, Redistribution. But as we noted in the last chapter, the wealthy have successfully made *redistribution* into almost a swear word that no responsible person, certainly no politician, would ever utter.

But with what has happened to us now because we ignored "the canaries," it's time we talk about it. To start with, there is a great religious tradition of redistribution in all the faiths. Caring for the poor and the needy through the giving of alms is one of the five pillars of Islam, a consistent theme through the Jewish Torah, and one of the most distinguishing characteristics of the earliest Christians.

The Torah carries a consistent theme that can challenge our thinking today. It is that we can never truly own the land: we only "rent" it for a while. Leviticus 25:23 says that "The land shall not be sold in perpetuity, for the land is mine; with me you are but aliens and tenants. Throughout the land that you hold, you shall provide for the redemption of the land." So not only is God the true owner of the land and we merely the tenants, but as tenants, we have a big responsibility. We are supposed to provide for the "redemption" of the land. The land could be used to grow crops, trees could be cut down to build houses, and the land could be mined for metal and stone, but those who were doing that work always had to keep in mind that they were also working for the good of the land, not just to maximize profit.

In addition to the reminder that we are not the true owners of the land came another mandate. Once every fifty years, any land that had been sold had to be returned to its original owner. "You shall hallow the fiftieth year and you shall proclaim liberty throughout the land to all its inhabitants. It shall be a jubilee for you: you shall return, every one of you, to your property and every one of you to your family" (Leviticus 25:10). It was a year when all debts were to be canceled, slaves were to be freed, land returned to its rightful owners, and families restored—a Year of Jubilee.

> IT WAS A YEAR WHEN ALL DEBTS WERE TO BE CANCELED, SLAVES WERE TO BE FREED, LAND RETURNED TO ITS RIGHTFUL OWNERS, AND FAMILIES RESTORED—A YEAR OF JUBILEE.

This mandate, if put into practice, would ensure that inequality would never be too great. This Jewish "public policy proposal" from the Hebrew Scriptures focused on promoting liberty through the freeing of those who were literally slaves to masters, those who were slaves to indebtedness and poverty, and those who were virtual slaves on land they worked as mere sharecroppers. Great poverty and inequality were seen as tyranny and one of the greatest threats to the liberty and freedom for which God had created his people. It was also through this regular, yes, *redistribution*, of land, wealth, and freedom that families were to be restored. And those who had gone away to find work could now return to the family's original land.

These redistributive practices were not an anomaly that happened only once a generation; they were supposed to be incorporated into the way landowners harvested their crops every season. Leviticus 19:9–10 instructs, "When you reap the harvest of your land, you shall not reap to the very edges of your field, or gather the gleanings of your harvest. You shall not strip your vineyard bare, or gather the fallen grapes of your vineyard; you shall leave them for the poor and the alien." This would ensure that everyone had the opportunity to eat and provide for themselves no matter how poor they were. These were not gentle suggestions about ways to give charitable gifts, but laws mandated for the good of the entire society. While we no longer live in an agrarian society, and we shouldn't try to pass a chapter out of the Bible through a Senate committee, the principles behind these laws reflect the very heart of God.

The earliest Christians made this kind of redistribution central to their identity. In the book of Acts, it says that "All the believers were together and had everything in common. Selling their possessions and goods, they gave to anyone as he had need." [1] As this early band of Christ's followers began to grow, they realized they would need a more sophisticated leadership structure. Their first act was to institute "deacons," whose job was to distribute resources to the poor. Already in the second century, the Greek Aristides wrote to Emperor Hadrian in C.E. 126 about the Christians:

They love one another. They never fail to help widows; they save orphans from those who would hurt them. If they have something, they give freely to the man who has nothing; if they see a stranger, they take him home, and are happy, as though he were a real brother.[2]

Emperor Julian, ruler of the Roman world for a short nineteen months in the mid-fourth century C.E., was frustrated in his failed attempts to reinvigorate traditional Roman religions by these same acts of charity. He said, "No Jew is ever seen begging, and the impious Galileans support not merely their own poor but ours as well."

FOUNDING FATHERS

This concern with inequality and mandate for redistribution, both through personal acts of charity and through laws governing property rights and social regulations, is certainly biblical—but is it American? Across the board, Americans believe not in equality of outcome but in equality of opportunity. Anger arises not because our country isn't perfect—because it never will be—but because many Americans believe we are not doing our best to live up to our ideals. When it comes to economics, to income and wealth, our country gives benefit to a small few to the detriment of most. America used to lead the world by leaps and bounds when it comes to opportunity; today, economic mobility is highest in Scandinavian countries, and studies suggest that it is higher in France, Canada, and Great Britain than in America.

> AMERICANS BELIEVE NOT IN EQUALITY OF OUTCOME BUT IN EQUALITY OF OPPORTUNITY.

Our Founding Fathers and the leaders of the American Revo-

lution are sometimes painted as simply antitax and antigovern-
ment fanatics. They weren't. Their rallying cry was against taxing
a populace that had little or no democratic input into their government. They were being ruled and taxed by an aristocratic and
wealthy elite that had little or no conception of the lives and
struggles of everyday people.

Thomas Jefferson, an avid defender of personal property
rights, made clear that he believed the government should
have a direct and active role in ensuring that everyone had
the opportunity to participate in the
economy. He argued in letters to
James Madison, "Whenever there is in
any country uncultivated lands and
unemployed poor, it is clear that the
laws of property have been so far extended as to violate natural right." He
advocated that the government provide small plots of land for free, con-
cluding with his famous statement,
"The small landholders are the most
precious part of a state." He never
advocated trying to attain a perfect
equality in outcome, but argued con-
sistently that inequality could undermine democracy and return the
United States to rule by an aristocratic
elite if the government wasn't proactive in preventing it.

> THOMAS JEFFERSON ARGUED CONSISTENTLY THAT INEQUALITY COULD UNDERMINE DEMOCRACY AND RETURN THE UNITED STATES TO RULE BY AN ARISTOCRATIC ELITE IF THE GOVERNMENT WASN'T PROACTIVE IN PREVENTING IT.

I am conscious that an equal division of property is
impracticable. But the consequences of this enormous
inequality producing so much misery to the bulk of mankind, legislators cannot invent too many devices for sub-

dividing property, only taking care to let their subdivisions go hand in hand with the natural affections of the human mind.[3]

James Madison, obviously convinced, argued for "the silent operation of laws which, without violating the rights of property, reduce extreme wealth towards a state of mediocrity, and raise extreme indigence towards a state of comfort." Always the radical, Madison even recommended withholding what he called "unnecessary opportunities" from some people if those opportunities would "increase the inequality of property, by an immoderate, and especially an unmerited, accumulation of riches."[4]

Thomas Paine, known as a revolutionary with a rhetorical flourish, said in the pamphlet *Agrarian Justice*, "It is not charity but a right, not bounty but justice, that I am pleading for. The present state of civilization is as odious as it is unjust. It is absolutely the opposite of what should be, and it is necessary that a revolution should be made in it. The contrast of affluence and wretchedness continually meeting and offending the eye is like dead and living bodies chained together." Paine recommended a 10 percent property tax in order to alleviate this inequality and argued that personal donations, while good, would never be able to solve the problem. Those that didn't want to pay the tax? "He that would not give the one (tax) to get rid of the other has no charity, even for himself."[5]

Our nation's founders were acutely aware that the concentration of wealth in the hands of the few came along with the concentration of political power in the hands of the few. Daniel Webster is quoted as saying, "The freest government cannot long endure when the tendency of the law is to create a rapid accumulation of property in the hands of a few, and to render the masses poor and dependent."[6] Either we can have democracy in this country or we can have great wealth concentrated in the hands of a few, but we can't have both. Remembering this simple principle could guide us to transform what, sadly, has become the status quo.

POPULIST OUTRAGE

Anger is a natural response to reading statistics like those in the previous chapter on how great the gulf between Americans has become. And anger in response to this kind of inequality, especially at great harm to the common good, is deeply embedded within our DNA. Sociologists and economists have devised and conducted experiments in cultures and countries across the world and found a common theme: that even in controlled experimental settings, there is an ingrained sense of fairness in the distribution of resources, and when a member of a community breaks out of those norms, anger and often redistributive actions are taken.

> WE CAN EITHER HAVE DEMOCRACY IN THIS COUNTRY, OR WE CAN HAVE GREAT WEALTH CONCENTRATED IN THE HANDS OF A FEW, BUT WE CAN'T HAVE BOTH.

In our country, this type of anger has often been referred to as "populist outrage." It has set loose angry mobs who have, on occasion, expressed their outrage through destructive behavior; but when channeled and focused, this outrage has also been behind great progress within our society. In response to rising inequality at the end of the nineteenth century, there was a growing social movement to improve the safety of working conditions and establish the eight-hour workday. The populist uprisings as a result of the Great Depression eventually led to the establishment of a minimum wage, child labor laws, and the establishment of Social Security.

The difference between blind rage and an effective anger is simple. Rage is a reaction defined and controlled by the injustices committed. It is a weak form of response because all that it knows how to do is lash out at what is wrong. In contrast, effective anger carries with it a vision of how things could change. Instead of simply decrying what is wrong, it shows the way forward to how things could become better. This is why, as I chronicled in my previous book, *The Great Awakening*, all of the greatest social movements that have led to great reforms have always had a deep spiritual component, usually rooted in faith.

PUTTING OUR BIBLES BACK TOGETHER AGAIN

While I was writing this chapter, I was sent a speech given that day, September 14, 2009, by Kevin Rudd, the prime minister of Australia. In the capital city of Canberra, the Australian leader was helping to launch a new Bible. I consider Rudd one of the most hopeful young political leaders in the world today, a committed Christian who seeks to apply his faith to his public service; we consider each other good friends.

He began his speech by recounting how an American president, Thomas Jefferson, had once cut out of the Bible every reference to miracles and the supernatural—because as a Deist, Jefferson simply did not believe those things. Then Rudd told the story of how our little group of seminarians had done a similar exercise at the beginning of Sojourners—cutting out every reference to the poor and to social justice in the Bible. Prime Minister Rudd said:

> The Jefferson bible, if you've ever seen it, is distinguished literally, waved in the breeze, full of holes. Jefferson, by the end of that exercise, was content with the document

he had produced. I thought this reflected a particular obsession, until I met Jim Wallis, from Sojourners. . . . When Jim Wallis began his work with *Sojourners*, a magazine which I still read, he and his colleagues then sat down . . . and again took out the Bible and decided to ensure that they would cut out all the references to God's injunction to social justice. And so they began, as it were, the reverse Jefferson exercise—cut, cut, cut, cut, cut—and again you have this Bible swinging in the breeze.[7]

I remember the exercise well, and it was one that fundamentally shaped the early sense of our own vocation and mission. I used to call it "our Bible full of holes," and we still have it in the office. We had to cut out a great deal, as the theme of poverty and social justice was the second most prominent in the Hebrew Scriptures (Old Testament). References to the poor and the requirements of justice are found in one of every sixteen verses in the New Testament, one of every ten in the first three books, the Synoptic Gospels, and one of every seven in the gospel of Luke.

I would take the shredded Bible out with me to preach, hold it high above American congregations, and say, "This *is* the American Bible, full of holes from all we have ignored and paid no attention to. We might as well all just take out our scissors, our Bibles, and start cutting." It was a dramatic challenge and made a powerful sermon illustration.

But now the British and Foreign Bible Society (known as the "Bible Society"), partly inspired, they tell me, by that almost four-decades-old story, has produced the *Poverty and Justice Bible* with the support of several other organizations, including World Vision and Micah Challenge—with all the passages about the poor and about social justice *highlighted*. And now, all the scriptures that ended up on the cutting-room floor after our formative seminary project are eye catching, in a vivid orange color. The color itself virtually says to you, "Pay attention to this."

Rudd went on: "Of course, the point of Jim Wallis and his colleagues was to demonstrate to the American Christian community at large that this was an incomplete document. If you excise what I understand to be thousands of references in both the prophetic literature of the Old Testament, and of course in the Gospels, the Acts, and the Letters, in fact you have a somewhat decimated document."

Rudd, who is an active Christian layperson with a special fondness for the German theologian Dietrich Bonhoeffer, reflected on the meaning of the new Bible to his diverse Australian audience:

> The Christian traditions from which you all come are many and varied. But I think all of you in this room would agree with one thing: it is not simply and exclusively some individual, pietistic retreat into yourself in pursuit of some microscopic spirituality. No, it's not that. It is a tradition alive in the fact that faith without works is dead, and that the Christian doctrine to which you all aspire, and which you all believe, is one that is both about individual spirituality and a parallel commitment to social justice.
>
> For me, the *Poverty and Justice Bible* is a sign of a new generation of Christians who are determined not to leave the Scriptures in pieces on the floor, but rather to live and act in ways that restore the integrity of the Word of God—in our lives, our families, our communities, our nation, and our world.

THE CHRISTIAN DOCTRINE IS ONE THAT IS BOTH ABOUT INDIVIDUAL SPIRITUALITY AND A PARALLEL COMMITMENT TO SOCIAL JUSTICE.

This Bible is a sign of how the faith community is changing—especially a younger generation of believers.

THINGS WE HAVE FORGOTTEN

I can't count the number of times, during this economic crisis, that somebody has said something to me about old values and lessons that they/we had somehow forgotten. Sometimes they recall the things they learned as a child from their parents or maybe in Sunday school, church, or synagogue or just the values that seemed to define the community where they grew up but have now disappeared. It's more than nostalgia; it's a feeling of loss. And they can't quite remember when and how they got away from those old values.

But three things are bringing the memory of those old values and lessons back.

First is the economic crisis itself. From middle-class families in debt up past their ears to CEOs who are finally finding the space for reflection, a fundamental reassessment may be taking place. And, of course, poor and working-class families are just trying to keep from completely drowning under the waves of recession. But many are now asking: is living with such economic aspirations and pressures what we really want, and what will give us the most ultimate satisfaction?

The second thing causing the soul-searching is a worry about what values our children are growing up with. It's not just money that people don't have enough of; it's time—and especially family time to be with their children. The demands of economic success have steadily eaten away at family time for many people, and the collapse of old economic assumptions and goals is focusing a spotlight on the empty personal and relational places in their lives.

Third, there may be a new empathy that emerges from all this for the poor and most vulnerable. All of a sudden many more people are vulnerable, close to the edge or falling over it. The judgments we have made about the poor may be slipping away as we see how fragile life is and how fast and easily things can go wrong, even for a family that is really trying. Hard times that hit middle- and working-class people can sometimes produce more compassion for all those who are most often left out and left behind.

So crisis creates openness and can open us up to learning and, sometimes, relearning, of old values. We are realizing now, for example, that when the economic gaps between us get too big, it is usually not a good thing for a society. Indeed, many of our economic crises have been preceded by great divides between the top and bottom of society. We are also realizing that our neighbors matter, and that our well-being is connected to theirs. Competing with the Joneses could be replaced with making sure that the Joneses are okay. And we might even learn why all of our religious traditions spend so much time talking about the poor and vulnerable—and why their well-being is seen to be one of the best tests of a society's integrity and "righteousness." Because when they are forgotten, the social bonds that hold the rest of us will soon be in jeopardy too.

PART FOUR

THE WAY OUT

8

ENOUGH IS ENOUGH

There is an old Shaker hymn that was played several times at Barack Obama's presidential inauguration. Its words are still beautiful as they teach us that " 'Tis the gift to be simple, 'tis the gift to be free." We have often been presented with a false choice: between a dull, drab, and deprived life or one of opulence and greed. Given our painful experience of the Great Recession, it's time to learn again that true freedom lies somewhere in between, where enough is enough. Our credit cards have become our chains, and debt our prison. We don't have to all become monks; Jesus always liked throwing a good dinner or party—he just wanted to make room at the table for those who weren't usually invited.

DON'T WORRY!

As I listen to Judy Collins sing that old Shaker wisdom in such soothing tones, I am also reminded of the words of Jesus in the Sermon on the Mount:

Therefore I tell you, do not worry about your life, what you will eat or what you will drink, or about your body, what you will wear. Is not life more than food, and the body more than clothing? Look at the birds of the air; they neither sow nor reap nor gather into barns, and yet your heavenly Father feeds them. Are you not of more value than they? . . . Consider the lilies of the field, how they grow; they neither toil nor spin, yet I tell you, even Solomon in all his glory was not clothed like one of these.[1]

Never were there more threatening, but also healing, words to a consumer society. Just before the Great Recession began, a full 70 percent of our economy was driven by consumption. If we are to learn anything from this crisis, it will be that such a level of consumer spending is simply not sustainable—not economically, not morally, and not spiritually. While I was working on this book, a good friend dropped by for a visit. When I told him what I was writing about, he launched into an eloquent and confessional commentary about how all of us, right across the political spectrum, had been consumed by our materialism. He is a leading political progressive, and not particularly religious, but his critique of what has now happened to most all of us was sobering. He spoke of the damaging consequences that our rampant consumerism is wrecking on the economy, the earth, the quality of our family life, and our very souls.

The United States, followed closely by Europe, has led the way in global consumerism, but now the new giant economies of China and India are poised to follow in our steps, creating a huge consuming middle class and adding new members to the club of the superrich. If, after the Great Recession, we return to our "normal" consumer habits, the impact will ultimately be more than the ecosystem of our planet, the ethics of our culture, and the inner life of our spirits can endure. A growing number of people, even some economists, are suggesting that a sustainable economy will be better built on producing things that are really needed (like clean energy, weatherizing millions of homes and businesses, better transportation, etc.) rather than relying on excessive and superfluous consumer items. And a lot of pastors and counselors would agree with this assessment at the spiritual level.

> IF WE RETURN TO OUR "NORMAL" CONSUMER HABITS, THE IMPACT WILL ULTIMATELY BE MORE THAN OUR PLANET AND SPIRITS CAN ENDURE.

The logic of a consumer society is fundamentally at odds with the teachings of Jesus. The relentless pressure of advertising tells us that "there is never enough" and that you should "worry" constantly about what you eat and drink, what you wear, whether your future is secure, and more. But Jesus said exactly the opposite. They say, "Please worry—all the time!" He says, "Don't worry!"

> Therefore do not worry, saying, "What will we eat?" or "What will we drink?" or "What will we wear?" . . . Indeed your heavenly Father knows that you need all these things. But strive first for the kingdom of God and his righteousness, and all these things will be given to you as well. So do not worry about tomorrow, for tomorrow will bring worries of its own. Today's trouble is enough for today.[2]

My friend Shane Claiborne asks a haunting question: "What if Jesus really meant the things he said?" It's an especially challenging question for the majority of Americans who say they are Christians. Is our allegiance to Jesus, or even respect for his teachings, strong enough to change our consumer habits, or are those now too "sacred" to tamper with? That will be one of the biggest questions coming out of the Great Recession. And in answering it, we have a great deal of help from our many reli-

gious traditions: The Christian tradi-

---~~~~~~~~~---
"WHAT IF JESUS
REALLY MEANT
THE THINGS
HE SAID?"
---~~~~~~~~~---

tion of Lent shows us we can live without things we thought we could not and reminds us of what we truly need. As we have already discussed, the Jubilee tradition from Judaism of-

fers a periodic leveling of the playing field: the forgiving of debt, the freeing of slaves, and the redistribution of land. In the principles of Islamic banking (which we'll look at in a later chapter), we can see examples of a healthy debt that is neither usury nor enslavement. As we work together and learn from one another, we can incorporate these time-tested principles into the way we live.

HOW MUCH WOULD MAKE YOU HAPPY?

According to a study by the wealth-management firm PNC Advisors, rich people almost never feel secure in their wealth. In fact, when they are asked how much they would need to feel secure, it is almost always twice their current net worth or income. That means that those with a net worth of $500,000 to $1 million said they needed $2.4 million. Those with a net worth of $1 million to $1.49 million said $3 million. And those with a net worth of $10 million or more said $18 million. Feeling financially secure, for those already rich—and I would suspect for most of us—is always subjective. It is always about having more than we already have. If our security and our happiness rests in our net worth, enough really never is enough.[3]

After spending so much time with millionaires and billionaires, with all the world's wealthiest elite, Robert Frank had this to say about the "Richistanis": "They're too young to retire, too driven to relax, and too concerned with keeping up with the next guy to live the storied life of leisure. In today's Richistan, even billionaires are rarely content."[4] For all of the fighting, striving, and sacrifice required for many of the world's richest to "arrive" in the world of Richistan, once they realize they've arrived, they are still so blinded by a desire to beat the person next door that they are never able to appreciate what they have accumulated. For those who always had wealth, they often don't know enough to realize what that enjoyment should be.

> IF OUR SECURITY AND OUR HAPPINESS RESTS IN OUR NET WORTH, ENOUGH REALLY NEVER IS ENOUGH.

WHAT IS THE GOOD LIFE?

Part of the unique nature of humans is that we are wired to look beyond how we *do* live and ask how we *should* live. With the great Greek philosophers, we always came back to the question "What is the good life?" We seek answers not just about how the world is, but how the world should be.

Rabbi Jonathan Sacks, Chief Rabbi of London, notes in his book *The Dignity of Difference* that we are looking for these answers in the wrong place. "Increasingly, we have moved to talking about efficiency (how to get what you want) and therapy (how not to feel bad about what you want). What is common to both is that they have more to do with the mentality of marketing (the stimulation and satisfaction of desire) than of morality (what we ought to desire)."[5]

He goes on to say, "Markets are by their very nature transactional, not moral. They are about prices, not values."[6] No matter how hard we look in the market for the answers to these deeper questions about life and its meaning, we will not find them there. That is not because the market is failing or because the market isn't doing its job well enough; it's just that the market is the wrong place to look for answers about morality.

David Hume spoke of this misguided quest as the "is-ought" fallacy. In his book *A Treatise on Human Nature*, he observed that many writers and thinkers inferred the way a thing "ought" or should be from the way that it "is." In other words, thinkers would describe how something is and then claim that is the way the thing should be. The compelling nature of faith lies significantly within its power to overcome exactly that line of thinking. It is the ability to honestly describe the way the world is, as messed up as it might be, and still believe in the possibility

> THE POWER OF FAITH LIES IN ITS ABILITY TO HONESTLY DESCRIBE THE WAY THE WORLD IS AND STILL BELIEVE IN THE POSSIBILITY OF A WORLD AS IT SHOULD BE.

of a world as it should be.

When times were good, keeping up with the Joneses meant consuming more and more—buying more stuff that we don't need with money we don't have. But what happens when the Joneses get their salaries trimmed or hours cut? What happens when the college savings plan crashes or the retirement account goes bust? It turns out that just as our neighbor's overconsumption can lead to our own overconsumption, so, too, can our neighbor's simplified life lead to our life's being simplified. Conspicuous consumption is only fashionable if we let it be.

"It's kind of like we all went overboard," a Ms. Taylor told the *New York Times*, "and we're trying to get back to where we should have been." In the same article, Maxine Frankel, a schoolteacher, said, "I think this economy was a good way to cure my compulsive shopping habit. . . . It's kind of funny, but I feel much more satisfied with the things money can't buy, like the well-being of my family. I'm just not seeking happiness from material things anymore."[7]

Stories like Maxine's are being reflected across the country. "Staycations" are keeping people in their own communities during their time off. Instead of expensive travel, families are taking the opportunity to stay at home and connect with one another and their communities and save a lot of money in the process. Things that once seemed essential have lost their grip, and proven unneeded luxuries are showing themselves as intrusions and obstacles to what is really important.

In another striking insight, Carol Morgan, a law professor at the University of Georgia, tells why she felt the need to cut excess spending. "Before, extravagance and opulence was the aspiration, and if we can replace that with a desire to live more simply—replace that with time with family, or time for spirituality—what a positive outcome to a very negative situation."[8]

THE WISDOM OF THE EARLY CHURCH FATHERS

This simplification is not a commitment to abject poverty but a change in priorities, a change in attitude. It is, I would argue, a choice to live more fully. Clement of Alexandria, an early church father, said that in the teachings of Jesus he found, "Not a command to fling away the substance that belongs to him and to part with his riches, but to banish from the soul its opinions about riches, its attachment

> SIMPLIFICATION IS NOT A COMMITMENT TO ABJECT POVERTY BUT A CHOICE TO LIVE MORE FULLY.

to them, its excessive desire, its morbid excitement over them, its anxious cares, the thorns of our earthly existence which choke the seed of the true life."[9] Simplicity in our living is not about having less of life; it is about having more of it. It is about clearing out the barriers that stop us from having it.

The theologian St. Augustine had this to say: "Greed . . . is not something wrong with gold; the fault is in a man who perversely loves gold and for its sake abandons justice, which ought to be put beyond comparison above gold. How could we feed the hungry and give drink to the thirsty, cover the naked and entertain the homeless . . . if each of us were himself already in want of these things?"[10]

St. John Chrysostom, Patriarch of Constantinople from C.E. 398 to 404 wasted no time when he challenged early Christians in his care about their wealth: "God in the beginning made not one man rich, and another poor. . . . He left the earth free to all alike. Why then, if it is common, have you so many acres of land while your neighbor has not a portion of it?"[11] His words would not test well in focus groups or make a good campaign slogan, but their challenge is a serious one.

A popular text used in the early church as a guide for living came from a Pelagian tract and gave this admonishment to early Christians: "Some people are indigent for the very reason that others hold a superfluity. Take away the rich man and you will find no pauper. No one should own more than is necessary but everyone should have what they need. A few rich people are the reason why there are so many poor."[12]

While those words were written nearly fifteen hundred years ago, they remain exactly the kind of questions we should be asking ourselves today. Is it wrong to have a nice house? No. But do we use that house to be more hospitable? Is it wrong to eat good food? No. But does that good food help us become more generous? Is it wrong to have clothes? A television? A computer? No.

No. No. But are we becoming more aware of the world around us and more compassionate toward it?

With everything we buy, we need to ask ourselves not only if we need it, but what type of person we are becoming when we buy it. Are we becoming more like the kind of human being we want to be, that we should be? Or does this purchase take us in the other direction?

> WITH EVERYTHING WE BUY, WE NEED TO ASK OURSELVES WHAT TYPE OF PERSON WE ARE BECOMING WHEN WE BUY IT.

REVEREND BILLY'S CHURCH OF STOP SHOPPING

In November 2007, theologian Walter Brueggemann profiled the prophetic acts and message of street performer, protestor, and preacher Reverend Billy in *Sojourners* magazine. While Reverend Billy is not an ordained minister and does not profess to be a Christian, he has founded the Church of Stop Shopping. It is an organization of activists and actors who use creative performance to question our culture of consumption and the large corporations sustained by it. The group uses street theater and has even "exorcised" some demons out of cash registers to make their point. These sorts of over-the-top actions, which drew attention to a mostly ignored societal ill, led Brueggemann to call him a "faithful prophetic figure who stands in direct continuity with ancient prophets in Israel."

Reverend Billy laid out his idea for a bailout in an interview with David Weidner of the *Wall Street Journal*—stop bailing out the mega financial institutions and focus on lifting up community banks and local neighborhood businesses. "It's hard to imagine Timothy Geithner taking advice from an iconoclast dressed in a white suit, clerical collar and Elvis-inspired hair, but the Reverend Billy may be on to something," the reporter wrote. For every dollar spent in a local community store, ninety cents stays in the community; for big chain stores only fifty cents stays.

Reverend Billy isn't what you would call a mainstream figure, and his message is not one that will usually be picked up by the mainstream media, especially not the nation's leading financial newspaper. But the same crisis that got me on a panel about the values of capitalism at the World Economic Forum got Reverend Billy's thoughts on economics in the *Wall Street Journal.* "Though colorful, Reverend Billy is no longer a fringe figure. Since he began preaching on the street corners in Times Square a decade ago, Reverend Billy and his anti-consumerism message have gained mainstream attention." [13] Crisis gives everyone a chance to rethink things and start asking some better questions.

> CRISIS GIVES EVERYONE A CHANCE TO RETHINK THINGS AND START ASKING SOME BETTER QUESTIONS.

DON'T HANG ON TO YOUR LUNCH

Is *Wall Street*'s Gekko right? Is it a zero-sum game? Does somebody have to win and another lose? We make the mistake of thinking that, because this is the way things are, it's the way things have to be. Day to day, many of us are finding that we don't need the things our neighbors have and that the things advertisements promise will bring happiness aren't necessary after all. There is a story in the Gospels that a lot of us learned in Sunday school about another kind of economic crisis. Jesus was teaching far away from any town, and a crowd of five thousand men plus many more women and children had gathered. As the day progressed, the disciples realized there wasn't any food for them. You might say their liquidity had frozen up in their food market and with everybody defaulting all at once, their CDSs (credit default swaps) didn't do them much good: "With all these thousands of people gathered, . . . hungry and ready for a meal, there was a little boy who came up and offered all that he had . . . five loaves and two fish."

When I hear this story, I try to imagine the disciples' reactions. They must have thought the boy's offering a comical joke. They were despairing of the problem and wanted Jesus to send the people home. "This is too big for us," they, in essence, said.

But God's economy is not our economy. God's reality is not our reality. Jesus took the small boy's offering seriously. He took the food and he blessed it. The disciples passed it out, and there was more than enough. So much so that there were twelve baskets of bread left over.

It's a miracle! Yes, but it was made possible by the little boy sharing his lunch and not just keeping it for himself. You see, his sharing gave Jesus something to work with.

There is an important lesson here for us. In an economic crisis, we all want to hunker down and hold on to our lunches. We want to make sure that we keep what we have because we are afraid that if we let go, even what we have will be taken away from us. However, God's economy teaches that when we share, things tend to multiply. And in God's economy we learn that what we think we know about the world is not how the world has to be.

> GOD'S ECONOMY TEACHES THAT WHEN WE SHARE, THINGS TEND TO MULTIPLY.

Why is the boy in the story even necessary? Couldn't God have just gone "Puff" and all the food they needed would just appear? Sure, but I now understand more about the crucial part the boy and his act of generosity played. His generosity gave Jesus something to work with. For God to act in our current crisis, he may also need something to work with—like the generosity and compassion of the people of God.

An extraordinary fact: guess which year in American history records the highest percentage of giving—to the church and to the poor—of any year, in inflation-adjusted dollars. 1933! Right in the midst of the Great Depression. And we have never seen such a percentage of giving ever since—even in the best of times. Difficult times can call out our best and most generous selves.

God's economy has two basic principles:

1. There is enough
2. If we share it

THE POOR ARE MORE GENEROUS

An article in *McClatchy News* caught my eye when it opened with the story of a man named Jody Richards. Jody saw a homeless man begging outside of a McDonald's in downtown D.C., a common sight that doesn't normally get a second look in this town. But Jody stopped and bought the man a ninety-nine-cent cheeseburger. Certainly a kind gesture, made even more significant when you factor in that Jody is homeless too, and that was a good 10 percent of the $9.50 he had earned that day from panhandling.

The author goes on to say, "The generosity of poor people isn't so much rare as rarely noticed, however. In fact, America's poor donate more, in percentage terms, than higher-income groups do, surveys of charitable giving show. What's more, their generosity declines less in hard times than the generosity of richer givers does." [14]

According to studies by Independent Sector, on average, the

poorest fifth of Americans always give at more than their capacity, the next two-fifths at capacity, and the wealthiest fifth are usually capable of giving two to three times more than they do currently. In tough economic times, the top four-fifths of Americans will decrease their giving anywhere from 32 percent to 45 percent; the bottom fifth only 23 percent.[15] According to the U.S. Bureau of Labor Statistics' survey of consumer expenditures, the poorest fifth of America's households contributed to charitable organizations at an average rate of 4.3 percent of their incomes. Compare that to the top fifth at less than half that rate, 2.1 percent.[16]

> THE POOREST FIFTH OF AMERICANS ALWAYS GIVE AT MORE THAN THEIR CAPACITY.

The *McClatchy* article goes on to quote many of these poor but generous givers, and their analysis of why charitable giving pans out this way is insightful.

Herbert Smith gives away 10 percent of his $1,010 monthly disability check and believes that, "We're not scared of poverty the way rich people are. We know how to get the lights back on when we can't pay the electric bill." Pastor Coletta Jones, of The Rock Christian Church in Southeast D.C., said "When you have just a little, you're thankful for what you have, but with every step you take up the ladder of success, the money clouds your mind and gets you into a state of never being satisfied."

Tany Davis, a laid-off security guard, had these insights: "As a rule, people who have money don't know people in need. . . . I believe that the more I give, the more I receive, and that God loves a cheerful giver. Plus I've been in their position, and someday I might be again." And this is the point. When you actually have poor people as friends and know their situations, you can't stereotype them and justify yourself by writing them off. Seeing, feeling, and knowing people in difficult straits is what creates empathy.

When enough is never enough and greed is good, our lives are in constant tension. There are always more toys to buy, more stuff to accumulate, and much more to worry about. The more we accumulate, the greater our fear and concern that it might all be lost. When we learn to be satisfied with what we have, when we let enough be enough, there is a satisfaction that creates time and space for other priorities in our lives like family, friends, and even—God. Just as the old maxim "Greed is good" needs to be replaced by the new/old virtue of "Enough is enough," we also need to find a replacement for "It's all about me." The alternative is: "We're in it together."

9

WE'RE IN
IT TOGETHER

There is a scene from the classic 1946 film *It's a Wonderful Life* that has become an enduring image of American community. George Bailey, played by actor Jimmy Stewart, with his wife (Donna Reed) and their five children, is gratefully smiling in the middle of his living room, surrounded by the borrowers of the town's credit union, which he runs, who are now bailing *him* out of trouble. It's a regular reminder and sentimental demonstration of one of our most deeply held values—that we are all in it together. We learn this from the biblical parable of "the welcome table," where we are all invited and reminded to also invite the poor and strangers to the feast, and from the biblical commandments to leave the edges of the field for the poor who are allowed to partake of the "gleanings."

What we are learning in the midst of this current crisis is that relationships really do matter. When the gaps between the rich and poor become too big, relationships are stretched thin and the old social covenants can't hold. The gospel story of the Good Samaritan teaches an age-old lesson that we must reach out to other human beings in need in order to be human ourselves and that we will likely have to cross some traditional social boundaries to do that.

Recognizing "our neighbor" in the one who is in need, especially if they are part of "the other" group, is a fundamental religious and moral value which must be radically recovered in a time of crisis such as this. A sense of community is still the foundation of a country, and even the global world we now live in. In the midst of this economic crisis, the poor are no longer "the others" from another group, they are now in our own neighborhoods and sitting next to us in our pews—and there are great lessons to be learned from that.

Our globalized world has flattened in ways we never thought possible, and we are learning just how connected we really are. We celebrate ethnic diversity, not because of guilt or political correctness, but because it is precisely through being with people who are not like us that we learn more about the richness of humankind and about who we truly are. Walls don't protect us from what is happening on either side of them. Everything from pandemic diseases, environmental degradation, global warming, the effects of poverty, and the violence born of extremism and despair all have a way of getting through, around, and past all the barriers we erect to protect ourselves. Now, more than ever, we can learn from the parable of the rich man and Lazarus. The rich man who ignored the poor man, Lazarus, who sat by his gate, was condemned not because he was rich, but because he ignored the humanity and very existence of the poor man.

> WE MUST REACH OUT TO OTHER HUMAN BEINGS IN NEED IN ORDER TO BE HUMAN OURSELVES.

SOUP FROM A STONE

The return to our oldest and best values could be a lot closer than we think. These values are not foreign to our lives or to the experiences and stories we tell; it's just that they have been crowded out. We have forgotten to apply them in the most obvious places.

Many of us remember the story of "Stone Soup." A stranger, carrying nothing but a large kettle and a stone, wanders into a town that is scarce on food and full of hungry children. The concerned villagers tell the man to move on, that there is no food to be found there. He is unconcerned and informs them that he has brought all he needs and that he will make soup from a stone. As he begins to heat the water and stir the pot, the stranger muses aloud that if only he had some potatoes the soup would be complete. Soon one of the villagers brings a few potatoes to add to the pot. Then the stranger remarks that onions would really complete the stew, and another villager brings some onions. Soon, the pot is filled with scraps and bits of food, everyone bringing what they could, and the soup is ready. Everyone eats and is filled.

It is a simple but important story—one that many of us heard as children and should be telling our children today. If given a choice between being the type of community that hordes scarce resources and one that shares what it can, which will we be? The stories we tell can give us a vision for the kind of community we want to be.

> THE POT IS FILLED WITH SCRAPS OF FOOD, EVERYONE BRINGING WHAT THEY COULD, AND EVERYONE EATS AND IS FILLED.

WHERE HAVE ALL THE GEORGE BAILEYS GONE?

The most sophisticated financial tools, the most well-paid executives in history, and some of the brightest minds are the ones who built the huge machines that just collapsed. Many small, local, and often "boring" banks survived and are much healthier. Why? The local bankers knew the people they were giving loans to, they knew the people whose money they were holding, and they understood the responsibility that involved, and so they avoided unhealthy relationships. Living down the block from those who were banking with them did more to help these bankers make wise decisions than all the high-paid executives and Ivy League graduates in the world could ever have.

The movie *It's a Wonderful Life* has been ingrained into our national psyche. Young and old know that "every time a bell rings, an angel gets his wings," and we all remember how Bedford Falls pulled together to support one another in the gravest of times. It is a story that represents America; it's about regular people living out all that is best about this country. It's a picture of a country that seems long gone, especially when you think of the banks then and the banks today.

While the picture seems long gone, not everyone has forgotten. I recently met one person who is keeping those principles alive and showing that they not only allow a bank to do well, they allow banks to do good. Ronald Hermance Jr. is the president, chairman, and CEO of Hudson City Bank in Paramus, N.J., which was established over 140 years ago. When banks across the country were engaging in risky mortgages, bundling them and then selling them off to Wall Street, Hermance stuck to the basics: getting to know his customers, taking deposits, and making good loans to those who wanted to buy houses. While foreclosures across the country continue to mount, Hudson City

Bank has maintained an astonishingly low default rate on home loans of just 1.05 percent.

I'm sure it was a temptation to change the bank's policies and loan practices when bank after bank saw skyrocketing profits. But Hudson City Bank kept true to its principles. Now, Ronald Hermance has been named the "Best Mid-Cap CEO" in 2008 by *Institutional Investor*, received the 2009 Corporate Social Responsibility award from the Foreign Policy Association, had his bank named the best-managed bank by *Forbes* in 2007 and 2008, and was given the inaugural "George Bailey" Banker of the Year award by none other than Jim Cramer![1]

Hudson City is the twenty-fourth largest bank in the country, but it has remained committed to the principles of small-town banking. While the big banks needed federal bailouts because they were deemed "too big to fail," Hudson City never needed a cent of federal money to stay healthy. When you hear Hermance talk about the pride he takes in hearing people call out to him, "Hey, George!" it's no secret where the success comes from. "We look to the lifetime of the relationship," he told me, "instead of just originating to sell." His bank originated all of its loans and then kept them all on their own books, instead of selling them off and letting someone else deal with them.

Across the country, many small banks that stuck true to their core values of service have been weathering the storm quite well. Many more, like Hudson City, have been doing better than ever. In one analysis of why small banks avoided so many of the devastating risks that took down or severely hurt the giants, it was the basic belief that our neighbors matter that kept them on track. The wealthy decision makers of the big banks thought they had all of the risk figured out and taken care of, while the little guys were concerned with the threat of embarrassment. As one news report put it, "They are run by people who grew up in the towns where they work, and their main fear is getting into a financial jam that will shame them in the eyes of their neighbors."[2]

The practice of giving someone a home loan and then dumping it off onto investors as soon as the papers were signed broke down a fundamental community relationship, and we are now suffering the consequences. There is a great difference between helping a fellow community member purchase a house and viewing a home-buyer as nothing more than the numbers represented on the contract he or she signs. The breakdown of this relationship caught up a lot of good people into a bad practice.

SHARIAH BANKING AND NEHEMIAH HOMES

In the midst of a tumultuous market, with home lenders dropping like flies and the world's largest banks in need of a bailout from Uncle Sam, University Bank in Ann Arbor, Michigan, recorded one of its best periods ever. Its growth market is Shariah-compliant mortgages. Shariah, or Islamic law, forbids giving out loans at interest or taking out loans with interest. So University Bank worked with the local Muslim community to develop a type of mortgage system that would comply with this requirement. Instead of borrowing the money from the bank and then paying back the capital with interest, the bank would buy the house, add a set fee, and then allow the home buyer to make monthly payments on the new total. Fariz Huzair, who bought his home with one of these mortgages, said, "In my heart, I'm doing this because it's the command of my Creator."

While the initial challenges for the bank were significant (they had to establish a board of Shariah scholars who could certify the mortgages as "halal," compliant with Muslim law), there have been very few defaults. Since the total cost of the house is clear up front, there is no room for the adjustable-rate mortgages, hidden fees, and additional costs that got so many people into houses they couldn't actually afford. Halal-certified mutual funds have sprung up across the country, and because they could not invest in the toxic mortgage-backed-securities pool, they have fared relatively well. Isam Salah, an expert in Islamic financing, was quoted as saying, "It's part of this religious revival, this return to roots, you see taking place not only in Islam but in many faiths." [3]

Some critics have pointed to banks like Hudson City and claimed that the only reason they have stayed afloat was because they only lent to wealthy customers. It was, these critics claim, low-income and poor people who tried to buy houses with debt they could not sustain who are at the root of this crisis. But Nehemiah Homes, founded by the community organizing group called East Brooklyn Congregations, has proven otherwise.

Nehemiah Homes was a project started by a group of pastors and community leaders in Brooklyn in the 1980s with a vision to rebuild poor and abandoned neighborhoods and create thriving communities where vacant lots once blighted the blocks. Selling exclusively to poor and working-class families, Nehemiah Homes Corporation can boast today a foreclosure rate of only 1 percent. Using innovative construction strategies, they kept costs low. And by recruiting large cash reserves from church denominations, they were able to give home loans to those who, at first glance, would not seem to be in the financial position to buy a home.

THE POTLUCK PERSPECTIVE

Just like the "Stone Soup" story that has been told over and over again throughout the years, another familiar practice reminds us of these same values. The church potluck is an old and cherished tradition in this country. Churches of all denominations and backgrounds ask their members to bring a dish to share with the rest of the congregation for a lunch or dinner they all eat together. Each person or family brings a salad, a main dish, or a dessert and lays it out on the table to share with everyone else.

There is, of course, always the person who fails to bring a dish but seems to eat the most. There are those who bring a full roast chicken cooked to perfection and those who bring a crunched loaf of white bread they picked up at the store on the way. There is the woman who has brought the same unpalatable-looking casserole that no one has yet to try for the past twenty years, and every once in a while everybody brings desserts.

The church potluck is almost always "unfair." People eat more than they brought or eat better food than what they offered. There are even the people who come expecting to bring nothing and leave all filled up. And yet, for generations, this tradition has survived and is even growing among a younger generation in their twenties.

A church potluck is not the American economy. I would never suggest that we try to run it as such. But this simple tradition does teach us a few lessons. *First*, in all aspects of life, there are always going to be times when things seem a little unfair and some people will try to get away with whatever they can. *Second*, most people, in their own way, want to contribute to the common good, and when that happens, there is always more than enough for all of us. We are learning that what is good for our neighbor is not just the right thing but is usually a good thing for us as well.

We are all hurt when we assume and expect the worst of our neighbors, when we live as if they are ready to take from us what we have left, if only given the opportunity. When we aim to separate ourselves from others, to act as solitary individuals, and to pursue our own selfish interests, we add fuel to the fire of our declining economy. But the lessons we learn in church, from potlucks and pulpits, can show us a better way.

> WHAT IS GOOD FOR OUR NEIGHBOR IS NOT JUST THE RIGHT THING BUT IS USUALLY A GOOD THING FOR US AS WELL.

THE GLOBAL IMPACT

As bad as things might get for us, World Vision, an international Christian aid and relief organization, recently gave me a reminder of just how bad things are for so many others across the globe.

Around the world, 126 million children are working in dangerous conditions. An additional 1.2 million are trafficked each year into forced labor, often as sex workers or child soldiers. World Vision workers around the world report increases of child labor in the countries where they work. As exports drop and factory jobs dry up, more and more people get desperate for any kind of work. "Recruiters" go into impoverished villages and promise parents good jobs for children and then keep them as virtual or literal slaves. Some families have little or no choice as their desperation comes from small debts often incurred from food, fuel, or medical costs, which they are unable to pay.

Jesse Eaves, World Vision's policy advisor for children in crisis, says, "Poverty drives people to desperate measures. And in dire situations, children become one of two things: a source of income or a drain on the income." In Cambodia, for example, 72 percent of children interviewed in brick factories are there because their parents cannot afford food, and 22 percent say their parents forced them to work to pay off debt.

> "RECRUITERS" GO INTO IMPOVERISHED VILLAGES AND PROMISE PARENTS GOOD JOBS FOR CHILDREN AND THEN KEEP THEM AS VIRTUAL OR LITERAL SLAVES.

Though these statistics are horrifying, the good news is that if we ensure that demand is decreased, the trafficking will decrease as well: "The key thing to understand with child labor," Eaves says, "is it begins and ends with you and me." He reminds us that "It's all about demand. We're part of the problem and part of the solution."[4]

The Catholic News Service reported on Pope Benedict's comments on World Food Day, October 16, 2008. The Pope argued that, even in times of scarcity, there are enough resources to feed all of the world's people; what we lack is the moral conviction to do it. How can such abundance exist right next to extreme deprivation? Because of the "race for consumption" that we still have not rethought even in the midst of scarcity. It is also fueled by the failure to "curb the selfishness of states or groups of countries or to put an end to the unbridled speculation that is affecting the mechanisms of pricing and consumption."[5]

We need to confront our culture of narcissism that says "It's all about me" with the alternative: "We're in it together." "It's not about you" is the opening line from Rick Warren's *The Purpose Driven Life* and it's simple wisdom we need to remember right now. Everyone is in need of a good neighbor, and each of us has the responsibility to be one in return. It is this responsibility to neighbors that saved some banks in our country from making the risky investments that helped contribute to the start of the Great Recession. It is through looking out for neighbors that some communities are rebuilding and making sure their friends and neighbors are getting through tough times. When we think about our actions not only in terms of how they affect us, but how they affect those around us as well, our actions end up being better both for ourselves and our neighbors. But it might not always seem that way in the short term; that is why we need to find a replacement for "I want it now." This replacement has much to do with looking to the benefit of future generations— even to the seventh generation.

10

THE SEVENTH-GENERATION MIND-SET

The original inhabitants of our country, the Native Americans, made important decisions by asking how they would affect the people and the land for the next seven generations. This is a far cry from quarterly profit-and-loss reports, and the single bottom line of stockholder benefit. We need to create *multiple bottom lines*, not just for assessing immediate profits but for measuring longer-term community and ecological impacts. And we need *multiple stakeholders*, including not only stockholders but also workers, consumers, the community, the environment, and future generations—even seven generations out.

Our aim must be to develop the ethic of a *sustainable economy* and sustainable communities and to teach that ethic to our children. From both the Christian and Jewish traditions, we learn the importance of Sabbath—allowing ourselves, our families, the land, and our communities the space and time for rest. Workaholism is affirmed and encouraged in our culture, but it creates habits that undermine healthy people, families, and relationships and that are, indeed, a new form of addiction. It's time to talk about the healing of our economic addictions.

Writing for the *Sojourners* blog, www.godspolitics.com, Elizabeth Palmberg pointed out a disturbing mentality that she referred to as "The Notorious I.B.G.," which stands for "I'll be gone"—a phrase all too often heard on Wall Street from the mouths of traders or bankers.[1] When looking at a deal or a market move that shows itself to be lucrative in the short term but risky in the long run, they fall back on a mode of thinking that the long term doesn't matter because, by the time disaster might hit—I'll be gone.

Economists refer to these "heads I win, tails somebody else picks up the tab" situations as "moral hazards." If you put an everyday person into a situation where he always reaps the benefits of the good decisions he makes but is little or not at all negatively affected by the bad decisions he makes—there isn't much incentive to make better decisions. When good people are in a bad system, those good people start making bad decisions.

> WHEN GOOD PEOPLE ARE IN A BAD SYSTEM, THOSE GOOD PEOPLE START MAKING BAD DECISIONS.

Many in Wall Street reaped great rewards during the success of their short-term bets, as managers and CEOs encouraged behavior that made their next quarterly profit report look strong. What was forgotten was that the decisions that make your next profit report look great, or even your profit report for the next few years look booming, are not always the decisions that will produce the results we all want, ten, twenty, or even fifty years down the line.

We saw the anger at these situations in Jon Stewart's confrontation of Jim Cramer at the beginning of the book. Millions of Americans who were planning long term put their money and their trust into the hands of others, whom they thought were thinking long term as well. Then it was revealed that many of those who were trusted with our retirement savings were not thinking about our retirement decades down the road, but only the next day's trade. From the now iconic crash of Enron to the fall of Lehman Brothers, we see the great destruction and harm this sort of thinking, if left unchecked, can cause.

Markets will always have ups and downs, bubbles will build and burst, business cycles will swing up and back down. Schumpeter, who warned about the market devouring society and then destroying itself, also reminded us that these natural cycles can fuel innovation and new sectors of the economy—they can provide benefits. It is beyond the scope of this book to delve into the difficult issues of who gets bailed out and who doesn't or the nature of business cycles, but it is clear that we must continue to ask questions about the I.B.G. "business as usual" mentality.

> MANY OF THOSE WHO WERE TRUSTED WITH OUR RETIREMENT SAVINGS WERE NOT THINKING ABOUT OUR RETIREMENT DECADES DOWN THE ROAD, BUT ONLY THE NEXT DAY'S TRADE.

SABBATH

To rest, to stop our labor and toil, is not a sign of weakness; rather, it reflects the very nature of God. The creation story in Genesis is clear about this: "On the seventh day God finished the work that he had done, and he rested on the seventh day from all the work that he had done. So God blessed the seventh day and hallowed it, because on it God rested from all the work the he had done in creation."[2]

Too often, our culture portrays those who need rest as vulnerable and weak, not having the strength to go on. The beautiful poem that makes up the introduction to the Torah and to the Christian Old Testament shows that rest comes out of a place of strength, not weakness. To cease from labor and enjoy and appreciate the work that you have done does not show a lack but rather a fullness.

> TO CEASE FROM LABOR AND ENJOY AND APPRECIATE THE WORK THAT YOU HAVE DONE DOES NOT SHOW A LACK BUT RATHER A FULLNESS.

Technology has increased the pace of our lives significantly. The efficiency benefits are abundant and clear, but the effects of those changes on the rest of our lives need to be examined as well. Are we able to enjoy dinner with our families as fully as we used to, with text messages, e-mails, and phone calls all popping up in our pockets? Are our times of recreation constantly interrupted by demands from the office? Do we get re-creation time at all?

SERVE AND PRESERVE

When it comes to using the natural resources around us, we have tended to ask the questions, "Is it possible and is it profitable?" But these questions have failed us. They have led to a mass overconsumption of resources and the destruction of many others. According to one historian, in the long history of the planet, we have had five great periods of extinction, and we are now entering a sixth.[3] The extinction rate of plants and animals is now proceeding at a thousand times the average historical rate. Statistics like these led columnist and author Thomas Friedman to ask, "What if the crisis of 2008 represents something much more fundamental than a deep recession? What if it's telling us that the whole growth model we created over the last fifty years is simply unsustainable economically and ecologically and that 2008 was when we hit the wall—when Mother Nature and the market both said: 'No more.' "[4] Sounds like prophecy to me, not just another op-ed column.

The earth has said "no more" before; in fact, much of the history of human civilization can be tracked by the rise and fall of cultures and empires that failed to think ahead in their use of natural resources. Ancient hunting societies that learned how to kill a mammoth were then able to feed their tribes. If they learned how to kill two with the same effort, they might be able to grow their tribes. But, archeological evidence shows, when they learned how to kill hundreds at a time by running them off a cliff, the tribe would grow quickly for a while and then collapse when the food source ran out.

The collective failure of the industrialized world to both regulate pollution and curb gross overconsumption has put billions of the world's poorest and most vulnerable people at increased risk of hunger, thirst, flooding, and disease. The failure of Christians to live up to the God-given mandate to serve and preserve the earth, what Genesis 2:15 calls "to till it and keep it," and be good stewards of the resources God has given us means an additional failure to live out God's mandate to care for the poor. We cannot claim to care for the poor while we turn our backs on our role in the destruction of the most basic resources our neighbors need for survival. Love for our neighbors and love for the planet on which our neighbors live cannot be separated.

> LOVE FOR OUR NEIGHBORS AND LOVE FOR THE PLANET ON WHICH OUR NEIGHBORS LIVE CANNOT BE SEPARATED.

According to the Intergovernmental Panel on Climate Change, the world's leading authority on the issue, an additional 40 to 170 million poor people are at risk of hunger and malnutrition this century; and 1 to 2 billion people, already in poor areas, could see further reduction in their water supplies. More than 100 million people could be affected by coastal flooding. And these dangers are not long off. In Africa, 75 to 250 million will face water scarcity by 2020, and crop yields could be reduced by 50 percent in some areas. All these changes could quickly produce a refugee crisis with as many as *200 million* displaced persons by 2050.[5]

Rt. Rev. James Jones, the Anglican bishop of Liverpool, is a church leader in England but has also become a global leader in the Christian responsibility to serve and preserve the earth. In a recent lecture he said:

> Just as we look back on previous times with incredulity and wonder how people, especially believers, could have not only condoned but succored the slave trade and slavery, so in later years I think subsequent generations, who will live consciously with the reality that the earth is not a limitless larder, will find it difficult to understand how we could have described ourselves so uncritically as: "consumers."[6]

Bishop Jones started as a skeptic about climate change and was not always convinced that his Christian faith had that much to say about taking care of creation. But he is not the only one who is changing his mind. Jim Ball, the founder of the Evangelical Environment Network, has described to me the uphill fight he used to have in churches to get Christians to pay attention to the environment. That, he says, has changed significantly over the past few years to a broad acceptance of the message of "creation care" and the direct connection that care for the planet has to include care for the poor.

According to a recent poll sponsored by Faith in Public Life and Oxfam America, 71 percent of Catholics and nearly two-thirds of white evangelicals believe there is solid evidence that the earth is getting warmer. Nearly eight in ten Americans and roughly the same percentage of Christians believe that we have an obligation to care for God's creation by supporting stricter environmental laws and regulations. Nearly seven in ten Americans and a similar number of Catholics and white evangelicals believe that climate change is making life harder for the world's poorest because of drought, famine, and crop failure; and even more of that same group—nearly three-quarters—support helping the world's poorest people adapt to these changes.[7]

It is little wonder that this change is taking place in Christian communities across the world. Ancient laws laid out in the Old Testament are explicit about creating ecologically sustainable economies.

THE LAND

Once a year, my wife, Joy, and I pack the kids in the car, throw in our suitcases, and make the drive from Washington, D.C., to my home city of Detroit. As we leave D.C., we run into the Appalachian Mountain range, winding through the hills of Virginia and then Pennsylvania. Slowly, the hills flatten out, and the plains of the Midwest begin. Before we reach Detroit, we drive past miles and miles of fields. Some of them are large squares of crops, lined by trees, and others are giant circles created by irrigation systems that spin water around from a central point, delivering it to the crops growing up from the ground.

We pass fields of corn, wheat, and soybeans, crops that pull up a lot of nutrients from the soil. After a few years of growing on the same plot of land, those nutrients become depleted; so to make sure that the soil is able to grow crops for years to come, farmers will change what they plant in a specific plot of land.

One year it might be corn that pulls lots of nitrogen from the soil, and the next year it might be alfalfa that returns nitrogen back to the soil, its "green manure." Some years they might just let a grass grow to give the land some time to rejuvenate and replenish itself. So as our family passes through this area, we also pass by some fields that don't seem to be growing much at all. The amazing thing is that these concepts are not just progressive agricultural theory, they reflect admonitions in the Bible about the proper use and care of the land.

Farmers have to employ the use of pretty complex chemistry and techniques, but the understanding that you have to let the land rejuvenate, that you can't just keep taking and expect the land to keep giving, is as old as farming itself. In fact, thousands of years ago, the Israelites had strict laws governing farming. Leviticus 25:3–4 says, "Six years you shall sow your field, and six years you shall prune your vineyard, and gather in their yield; but in the seventh year there shall be a sabbath of complete rest for the land; a sabbath for the Lord: you shall not sow your field or prune your vineyard."

If you are only thinking about the year ahead of you, this doesn't make any sense! In fact, it sounds crazy! In an ancient society that wasn't shipping in food from around the world, the idea of going an entire year without planting your fields sounds like a recipe for disaster. But when you take the long view, when you are not just thinking about the here and now, but are also looking to the future, it's not a crazy idea at all. In fact, it's crazy not to do it. Farmers know that if you grow as much as you can every year in the same soil, without giving it a break and letting it replenish its nutrients, you have a recipe for disaster! Each year as the nutrients diminish, your

> JUST BECAUSE THERE IS A CLEAR BENEFIT NOW DOES NOT MEAN IT IS A GOOD CHOICE.

crops will be less healthy and your harvest less abundant. If you never give the soil a break, if you don't think about the long-term health of the land, eventually you won't be able to grow any crops at all.

And these principles about the land apply to the rest of economics as well. When we make choices about using natural resources, we need to remember that just because the things we do are possible does not mean they are right. Just because there is a clear benefit now does not mean it is a good choice. Even though we can do something does not mean we should.

THE NEXT GENERATIONS

With all the immediate demands on our time and attention, it can be difficult to think about the days ahead, let alone future generations. Nonetheless, it is a challenge we must all try to meet. My adult life has been committed to a ministry of calling Christians to the message of social justice, which is at the heart of the gospel and the life and ministry of Jesus. At my organization, Sojourners, we sum it up in just a few words: "Faith in Action for Social Justice." What consumes a significant amount of my time and attention are the day-to-day and month-to-month plans of the organization, our mission, and our goals. But I also work hard to keep an eye on what is to come for future generations.

A few years ago I hired a young assistant, Chris LaTondresse. When I met Chris, he was a student at Bethel College and organizing his fellow students around issues of poverty and justice. Chris traveled with me across the country, and we talked on long plane rides and frequent car rides. He sat in on meetings and listened at all my speaking engagements. He supported me with feedback, especially ideas and perspectives from a younger generation. His support to my work was invaluable, and our time together also helped give him the training and experience that he is now able to apply to his duties as the U.S. director of a non-profit that does development work in the Middle East.

While Jesus kept a busy schedule throughout his entire ministry, he spent time with the next generation of leadership who would take up the mantle of his cause. For us—pastors, business leaders, and politicians—it is of the utmost importance that we take time away from the immediate, and even from our own work, to think about the next generation of leaders who will be here long after we are gone. The more we can do to invest in them now, to give them experience and opportunities, even if that means we "get less done" right now, the better for them and for our collective future. When it comes to seventh-generation thinking, we should be judged not only by what we accomplish in the now, but by the quality of the leaders we raise up for the future.

THE NEED FOR HEROES

The upcoming generation that is closest to my heart is that of my two sons, eleven-year-old Luke and six-year-old Jack. Having children forces me to think about the future and what the world will be like in years to come, long after I am gone. I wonder what kind of world we will leave behind, but also what my children will think of my generation and our legacy. While there will always be villains, I hope my children will find many heroes to follow as well.

When my son Luke was in fifth grade, he had a homework assignment to research and discover someone he considered a hero and explain why. So he Googled several of his heroes, printed out their pictures, made the pictures into badges, and put them on the backpack he carried around every day. The result was a ten-year-old boy carrying around photo badges of

Nelson Mandela, Martin Luther King Jr., Dorothy Day, John Lewis, Jane Goodall, Bill Gates, Jackie Robinson, Sojourner Truth, Desmond Tutu, Mahatma Gandhi, William Shakespeare, Barack Obama, and, of course, LeBron James! My kindergarten son had his heroes too: he donned his walls with Spiderman, Superman, Batman, and Robin; and he imagined himself saving the world as they do each and every day.

Who children admire is important because it affirms and shapes a particular set of values. We want their heroes to represent compassion, courage, service, and sacrifice, as opposed to self-interest and self-protection. Celebrities are role models, for good or ill, and that's why we need more of them to be heroes and not just celebrities.

> WHO CHILDREN ADMIRE IS IMPORTANT BECAUSE IT AFFIRMS AND SHAPES A PARTICULAR SET OF VALUES.

I have been pleased to overhear conversations between my ten-year-old son and his fellow Little League baseball players, many of whom I also coach, when they evaluate the ethics of their baseball heroes. It's been encouraging that the stats of our best-known athletes are not the most important thing to these young players; it's also how they behave and live off the field or court. Taking performance-enhancing drugs is enough to get the big-name athletes written off as "cheaters" by my son and his friends (which I, frankly, agree with), and what their favorite stars do to help other people is as important as their home runs and slam dunks. I will always be grateful for a fifth-grade teacher who asks his students to define their heroes.

PART FIVE

NEW HABITS OF
THE HEART

11

THE CLEAN-ENERGY ECONOMY CONVERSION

America is a global leader, and for better or worse, countries across the world follow our lead and emulate our behavior. But if the entire world begins to consume at the rate Americans currently do, the planet simply cannot sustain us. The earth is already groaning from our current levels of global consumption, and if the rest of the world follows our lead, the results will be disastrous. That's the bad news.

But here's the good news. The change to a new "green" or clean-energy economy could accomplish three things simultaneously: (1) protect the planet by beginning to mitigate and even reverse climate change; (2) create new and better jobs (and ones that can't be exported to other places); and (3) serve our national security by changing the single factor that has led us into one war after another—our dependence on oil.

But the change from a fossil-fuel-driven economy, society,

and culture to a newer clean-energy economy will require a fundamental transformation—from the way our energy grid is wired to the ways we are wired. It will take far more than just a change in the energy system; it will also take a *change of heart.* Such a transformation will entail more than just research and investment in new clean-energy sources; it will require a change of old habits and lifestyles into new ways of thinking and behaving, a whole new orientation and direction—in short, nothing less than *a conversion.*

An economic *conversion,* a word that even economists use when talking about this change, will also require a personal conversion of our hearts and minds. The issues at stake here are so momentous and potentially transformational that such a conversion will have to be both economic and *spiritual.*

> NEEDED CLEAN-ENERGY CHANGES WILL REQUIRE NOTHING LESS THAN *A CONVERSION.*

The other good news is that change is already happening. It is especially happening with a new generation of young people. In other words, the conversion we need is indeed both structural and spiritual, but it must also be *generational* if we are to accomplish such a major shift.

URBAN KIDS

Let me get personal for a moment here. I was an urban kid, born and raised in Detroit. My undergraduate schooling was in East Lansing/Lansing at Michigan State University and seminary in Chicago, building community in the poorest neighborhoods. For more than three decades, I have lived in Washington, D.C., most of the time in the inner city where we hear gunfire most every night. My wife, Joy, was raised in the tough urban neighborhoods of South London where her dad was an Anglican priest and where, after theological school in the beautiful city of Durham, she came back to be an urban priest herself. Our two boys are urban kids too, born and raised in the inner city of D.C., going to the most racially and culturally diverse elementary and middle schools in the city, playing baseball and soccer on the urban playgrounds and ball fields of the nation's capital.

I am writing this on a beautiful island—Block Island, off the coast of Rhode Island. I used to come here years ago to visit William Stringfellow, who came here from New York City after he got very ill and who was a Harvard Law School graduate turned storefront lawyer. He was part of one of the first urban Christian communities in the country—the East Harlem Protestant Parish. I remember coming here as a young activist from the city, and I recall it being a dramatic change from the life I was used to in the city—an almost monastic experience that forced me to radically adjust my pace to the very different cycle of island life. I also came to visit Daniel Berrigan, who was arrested for his Vietnam protests here at the Stringfellow house by FBI agents posing as bird watchers. That's about the only way you could go unnoticed here—by looking like a nature lover and observer.

Stringfellow, the lawyer and lay theologian who wrote so eloquently about faith and politics, also got involved in the politics of the island, becoming for a time the warden (mayor). He especially focused on fighting the developers who threatened the life and pace of the island, and he is now viewed as one of the fathers of the environmental movement here—which has succeeded in protecting 43 percent of its beautiful habitat from further encroachment.

I brought Joy Carroll out here when we were dating and eventually proposed to her at the sandy point of the North Light, which has some of the most beautiful sunsets in the world. To my great blessing, she said yes, and now our family has been coming here for a couple of weeks in the summer to stay at the "Berrigan cottage" on the Mohican Bluffs, facing the Atlantic Ocean. Of this cottage, Dan Berrigan wrote: "At Land's end, where this house dares stand, where the sea turns in sleep ponderous, menacing, and our spirit falls and runs landward, seaward, askelter . . ." The poem graces the wall of the cottage it describes.

When we are here, our morning routine includes my taking the two boys on the activities sponsored by the Nature Conservancy, which include hikes and scavenger hunts for amazing things; "marsh mucking" where we find hermit, fiddler, and horseshoe crabs and all manner of shells; bird watching and banding; walks through hollows, along cliffs, and into enchanted forests; and even, once, quietly sitting together long enough to actually watch a monarch butterfly break out of its cocoon and enter the world. For us urban kids, this is a transformation of mind, heart, lifestyle, pace, and consciousness.

I have noticed how easily my two boys take to this. They soak up every word of the college-age nature guides who meet and instruct us each morning and can repeat back information and facts much better than I can. They are amazed and animated by it all. And I notice, even back in our home environs of Washington, D.C., they are much more environmentally conscious than either of their urban parents. They easily "get" recycling, are focused in picking up litter and trash, are very critical of big gas-guzzling vehicles, and believe conservation is the right thing to do. And most of their young friends are the

> OUR BOYS ARE MUCH MORE ENVIRONMENTALLY CONSCIOUS THAN EITHER OF THEIR URBAN PARENTS.

same way—even in the city. I overhear them talking to one another about environmental things at baseball practice when I am coaching Luke's and Jack's teammates in Little League.

Eleven-year-old Luke regularly starts conversations on topics of environmental responsibility and simply doesn't understand people and politicians who just don't get it. And the other day, six-year-old Jack announced that when he grows up, he is going to invent something that will help the environment (he and his mom had been working to create a compost pile outside the house). Having only one car, using less gas, installing energy-saving light bulbs, and "not hurting the environment" seem to all come naturally to them. They also think that since God cares about the environment, we should too.

LIVING GREEN

That greater environmental consciousness is, of course, spreading throughout the country and the world, especially among the young, and the economic crisis seems to have greatly accelerated the concern. Already, people are using less gas, carpooling more miles, and cutting back on unnecessary trips. Just over the course of 2008, gasoline consumption dropped 6 percent.[1] It's an important shift, given that in some areas of the United States up to 50 percent of greenhouse gas emissions come from passenger vehicles.[2] Much of this was because of a changing economic reality, but the shift does not need to be temporary. Once people learn that they can live by driving less and carpooling more, they will do so in the future even without the economic demand.

Entire towns in Germany are now being built with one big rule: you can't drive a car in the community. In Vaubun, Germany, 70 percent of the families do not own cars and 57 percent sold a car to live there. Heidrun Walter, a resident of the community, said, "When I had a car I was always tense. I'm much happier this way."[3] While many of our nation's suburbs were designed with two-car families in mind and with shopping and business centers removed from housing, more and more developments in the United States and Europe are being designed with a "low-car life" in mind. Housing developments here in the United States are being built with common areas, shared pools, communal lawnmowers, and regular potlucks. New communities are being created by younger people of faith, based on a more "simple way."

> MORE DEVELOPMENTS IN THE UNITED STATES AND EUROPE ARE DESIGNED WITH A "LOW-CAR" LIFE IN MIND.

Giving up driving altogether might not be feasible for many people, but more and more are giving up car ownership. Zipcar, a national car-sharing service, allows city residents to make use of a car only when they need it. Members pay an annual fee and then can sign up online to use cars parked throughout their neighborhoods or the entire city. Gas and insurance are included!

Zipcar was started by Robin Chase, a forty-two-year-old mother of three. A *New York Times Magazine* article reported, "Car sharing, Chase thought, was an ideal way 'to harness the engine of self-interest' for the good of all." She realized that this model was an excellent way to provide a service that people needed—"wheels when you want them"—and reach a goal she believed in: fewer cars on the road. She said, "I'm gleeful about the engine of capitalism, but it has some very negative, destructive aspects. We see it around us now: extreme greed. Shocking arrogance." Since its start, Zipcar has nearly doubled in size every year.[4]

When it comes to a green economy, we are used to being told that we have to choose between jobs and the economic well-being of our children and survival of the planet for our grand-children. But this crisis has shown that not to be the case. It is increasingly clear that the world's next big industries and areas of job growth will be lessening our impact on the environment.

Author and activist Van Jones describes in his book, *The Green Collar Economy*, how green jobs tackle two of our world's greatest challenges—poverty and the environment. Weatheriza-tion of buildings can save both businesses and homeowners money and create jobs that can't be exported. Installing solar panels and "green" roofs can help cut down on our waste, and they are also jobs that will start here and stay here. In Chicago, ex-offenders released from prison are trained in computer repair so that old computers can be recycled and used in schools serv-ing students from lower-income families. Urban farmers are cleaning up toxic soil, growing produce in vacant lots, and sell-ing it at farmers markets. Houses, instead of being destroyed, are being disassembled and their parts resold.

Writing for *Sojourners* magazine, Jeannie Choi described part of the transformation occurring in the Rust Belt city of Pittsburgh: "Abandoned factories along the waterfront and boarded-up stone chapels stand like ruins, reminding residents of what once was. Today, the city has more than 14,000 vacant lots."[5] But that's not the end of the story. A new startup com-pany called GTECH—Growth Through Energy and Commu-nity Health, is transforming these empty lots by planting sunflowers and harvesting them for the production of bio-fuel. The city is adding beauty, and we all benefit from the growth of alternative fuels.

We had a chance to make the shift after the 1973 oil em-bargo, when the United States turned its focus for a few short years to fuel efficiency and alternative energy. Congress passed a fuel-efficiency mandate for automakers of 27.5 miles per gallon that took full effect in 1985. Instead of continuing on this track, President Reagan rolled it back to 26 miles per gallon in 1986. He also slashed the budgets of most of the alternative-energy programs that had been started, and he defunded much of the Solar Energy Research Institute. The Democratic-controlled Congress at that time let the tax incentives for solar and wind startups lapse. Many of the U.S.-based companies that started up in response to the public-sector investment and tax credits given to jump start the industry were then sold to companies in Japan and Europe. In 1979, President Carter had ordered that solar heating panels be installed on the roof of the West Wing as an example to the country. In 1986, President Reagan had them removed.[6]

In 2009, President Obama signed new regulations to increase fuel economy. But even with the new standards, the United States is still falling behind. By 2016, the average U.S. vehicle should get 35.5 mpg, a 40 percent increase over today. But today, the Japanese standard is 42.6 mpg, and the European is 43.3 mpg.[7] We clearly still have a long way to go.

These changes will not be easy, and some might even require sacrifice. Changes in environmental policy often hurt the wallets of poor people first, and responsible policy should always take that into account—mitigating the impact on low-income people. But just because conversion can be a challenge doesn't mean it is not worth doing and doesn't mean that, down the road, it won't pay off. Rich Cizik, longtime evangelical Christian leader and president of the New Evangelicals, wrote, "And when we die, God won't ask us how He made this Earth or how long it took, but instead this question about our stewardship duty: 'What did you do with what I made?'"[8]

People are learning to share out of short-term economic necessity and hopefully will keep sharing for long-term sustainability. New habits of the heart that are formed in times of need or out of necessity can turn into patterns for a lifetime. The change to a green economy would be one of those big changes that would begin to change everything else—it would be a conversion.

12

THE FAMILY
MATTERS CULTURE

There has been a war declared on our families, but it has not come from the places and people we have been warned about. It has rather been fought in longer hours, reduced paychecks, distorted measures of success, a relentless pressure to keep up with the Joneses, and a cultural onslaught directed against our children, promoting some negative values that most of us don't want our kids growing up with.

We need to ask: what makes a healthy family? The latest and the greatest can become the enemy of family and friends. Parents struggle with wants versus needs, reading time versus screen time, and encouraging imagination versus simply providing entertainment.

The time we spend with our spouses and children is the key investment we make in our most important legacies. For example, how can the values best learned in our religious congregations, service organizations, or Little League stay with our children for the rest of their lives? How do we teach our children the values of compassion, fairness and equality, human dignity, social justice, and community? Few things are more important.

LITTLE LEAGUE

One of the most important family commitments I make is my time coaching both my sons' Little League baseball teams.

"Dad, could we go to the field and practice a little more pitching?" Our Astros team had just won the Northwest Washington, D.C., AAA championship game in the last inning. The kids and parents were all excited, and we had just finished the big postgame and end-of-season party at our house—passing out trophies and pizza. Everyone else had gone home, and Luke, my son and dependable cleanup hitter and closer pitcher, wanted a little more baseball. "Sure," I said with a smile. "Let's go!" What else can a coach, and a dad, say?

It was a very short walk, which is why our family moved to live on the edge of Friendship Field in Turtle Park. I think it's the best baseball field in the city, with four adjacent diamonds on this field of dreams. For a baseball family like ours, this is like living on the beach. And this is where our sons, Luke and Jack, will spend much of their next several years.

There was nobody else on any of the four baseball fields, because by this time it was almost dark. So we chose the one on which we had just won the big game. Luke walked to the mound, and I bent over as best I could to be his catcher. But it wasn't many pitches before I said, "Luke, if we keep pitching in this darkness, one of us is going to get hit in the head, and it will probably be me! Let's just go for a walk around the fields and talk about the game." Luke thought that was a great idea.

So two guys, a father and son, slowly walked around all of Turtle Park in the dark, making sure to carefully touch home plate on all four fields. We talked about baseball and other stuff.

At the end of the walk, as we were heading home in the darkness to the guiding and welcoming lights of our house, my son looked up at me and said, "I love you, Dad." And suddenly the whole world was just about perfect. When we got back, I was surprised to see little Jack still up. But he met us at the door and said, "Dad, could you and me practice pitching tomorrow? I'm getting pretty good!" My morning had just been planned.

> MY SON LOOKED UP AT ME AND SAID, "I LOVE YOU, DAD." AND SUDDENLY THE WHOLE WORLD WAS JUST ABOUT PERFECT.

A GROWING HUNGER FOR FAMILY VALUES

Across the political spectrum, there is a new hunger for family values, and all the data show that strengthening the family changes the indices for all kinds of societal well-being. Stronger families solve a myriad of social problems, and the bonds of family are among the things that bring us the greatest satisfaction. A culture based on family matters, where the ethics of sustaining families is more important than market values, would be an enormous change in our habits of the heart—another conversion.

Deep concern over what is happening to our kids seems to be an almost universal issue among all of us—rich, middle-class, and poor; every race and religion; and those with diverse political views. Even when people are not practicing positive values in their own lives, when they become parents, they are quickly concerned that their children do. Among those incarcerated, for example, concern for their children seems to be almost universal, and continued connection to their children turns out to be one of the most predictable measures of prison behavior and lower recidivism rates upon release. Faith-based ministries that focus on connecting the children of incarcerated people (one of the most vulnerable of all populations) to their parents in prison report the most remarkable, humanly touching, and very practical sets of results.

As people lose their economic security, their jobs, their homes, and of course, their investments for the future, they worry about the impact these losses will have on their children. Of course they worry about their children's health, safety, and future; but a growing and very real concern is for the *values* of their children in a society of runaway consumption, debt, and selfishness. Parents are concerned that our society places much higher values on material things than it does on spiritual or even human concerns. In particular, they are concerned about how the market values and economic pressures have crowded out family time.

I've had many conversations with low-income mothers who must work multiple jobs and countless hours just to keep food on the table and a roof over the heads of their children. They are often in tears as they tell me the most painful thing about their demanding work schedule—not being there to put their children to bed at night.

But most middle- and even upper-middle-class households are also feeling the squeeze of time and money, even households with two parents. They now have to maintain two jobs outside of the home, which makes the juggling of work, school, after-school activities, sports games and practices, birthday parties, family meals, and family time increasingly difficult. What suffers most under extreme economic pressure are the old and traditional family values that place raising children well at the center of life. And that loss is being felt across the entire economic spectrum.

ENTERTAINMENT AND EDUCATION

In doing the research for this book, I noticed some things that I hadn't before. One of them was the contrast between the steadily declining prices of so many consumer goods, especially in the electronics and entertainment industries, and the dramatic rise in the cost of things like education.

When color televisions were first introduced in the late 1950s, the average set cost $2,227 in 2000 dollars; the cost was cut in half by the late 1960s, and in the year 2000, the average set cost $175. Today, with a little bargain hunting, a small LCD flat-screen television will set you back only $200, and those old models are almost being given away. Microwaves would cost the equivalent of $1,300 in 2000 dollars back in 1955, but in the late 1960s, only $495. Today, they can be found in many college dorm rooms across the country with models selling for under $50. In less than a lifetime, computers have gone from giant machines, taking up entire rooms and only within the reach of large corporations, the government, and a handful of elite universities to being almost everywhere and entirely commonplace. Netbooks (tiny laptops designed just to connect to the Internet) have computing power beyond what most of us could have imagined just a few decades ago, and they still sell for under $300. Other laptops that cost less than $100 to manufacture have now been designed by nonprofits and are being distributed in some of the poorest villages across the world.

While some costs have continued to drop, other costs have continued to rise. Tuition plus room and board for the average degree-granting public institution, for the 2007–2008 school year, was $11,600; and for a private institution it was $29,900 dollars. If those students' parents were in school just thirty years earlier, for the 1977–1978 school year, the same costs in real dollars would have been $1,900 for public institutions and $4,200 for private ones. While many of these costs may be worthwhile expenditures because of increased future earning potential, it is still alarming that the average collage graduate now leaves school with $21,900 in student-loan debt.

Think about it. What gets cheaper and cheaper is looking at screens—flat-screen televisions, computers, cell phones, and BlackBerrys—and listening to music on iPods and other portable devices. Watching, listening, texting, e-mailing, and cell phoning are all things that keep us busier and busier but also less connected to family and to one another. As I have heard from parents of many college-age students, they sign up for Facebook to find out what their kids are up to, because they certainly aren't using their cell phones to call home more often.

> THINK ABOUT IT. WHAT GETS CHEAPER AND CHEAPER IS LOOKING AT SCREENS—FLAT-SCREEN TELEVISIONS, COMPUTERS, CELL PHONES, AND BLACKBERRYS.

At the same time, education for our children—one of the highest priorities for all parents—is costing us more and more and putting us and our children into crushing, choice-limiting debt. While parents and students struggle to keep pace with the skyrocketing costs of education, we see a different set of priorities in state spending. Over the past two decades, states have increased their spending on corrections systems by 127 percent while spending on higher education has only increased 21 percent. In some areas of the country, spending on community colleges has often failed to keep pace with inflation. Community colleges provide valuable vocational training and access to higher education for low- and moderate-income people, as well as those looking for inexpensive alternatives for furthering their education.

THE BIG SQUEEZE

My heart broke in March 2009 when I saw the unfolding of a "kids for cash" scandal in Wilkes-Barre, Pennsylvania, as two juvenile court justices were arrested for accepting $2.6 million in payoffs over the course of six years in exchange for locking up kids. How did this work? PA Child Care LLC, and its sister company, Western PA Child Care LLC, are the privately run prisons that these youth were being sent to. If juvenile crime rates decreased in Pennsylvania, or youth were spending less time in detention facilities, the bottom line of these companies would be hurt; but the more kids going to prison, the higher the profits. So now the market has found a way to make locking up our nation's children a profit generator.

America's burgeoning middle class, and the opportunity for many to enter it, used to be the envy of the world. But our middle-class economy has now turned into an hourglass economy. The rich are richer at the top, the middle-class families get squeezed in the middle, and those at the bottom are crushed by the weight of it all. So here is how the new economy works: high consumption at the top end; high pressure for consumption in the middle, squeezing both money and time; decreased jobs and wages at the low end, causing growing poverty and leading to more incarcerations—which increases demands for a growing sector of for-profit prisons. It's all working quite well after all!

> THE MARKET HAS FOUND A WAY TO MAKE LOCKING UP OUR NATION'S POOREST CHILDREN A PROFIT GENERATOR.

These pressures are only a part of the story. I also see parents struggling to make their families a priority again, but this choice doesn't make sense when viewed from a market perspective.

Most parents in audiences I speak to quickly begin nodding their heads when I say that parenting is a countercultural activity. Joy calls our collection of families from school, soccer, and baseball "the village"—and in many ways, she has become "the village priest" in her relationships to many of those people. She enjoys being so involved in the boys' school and even loves running the school auction, shamelessly getting all our friends to donate stuff (the most recent example was getting Bono to autograph two school T-shirts!). She recently did a wonderful commencement address at Goshen College in Indiana and inspired the eager young graduates to make their lives really count for something.

I am very blessed to have a wife and partner with whom to share a common vision of faith and justice and an even deeper understanding of the things that make life rich, human, and good—an ongoing conversation that is usually shared over a glass of wine at night. And if my priest wife is ever to go back to pastoring a church, it would likely have to be called Grace Church, because she has the deepest theology of grace of anybody I know—a gift that comes in very handy with a husband like me who regularly needs the blessing of grace.

Good corporate and public policy can also make a difference for many families. Take, for example, leave policies. A recent study by the Center for Economic and Policy Research (CEPR), considering U.S. companies of all sizes and workers of all tenures, found the norm to be nine days of paid vacation with six days off for public holidays, a total of fifteen days. It also estimates that almost one in four U.S. workers doesn't get any paid days off at all. In contrast, another study by a human-resource consulting firm of other countries, showed much more generous policies. All members of the European Union must provide workers with a minimum of twenty paid vacation days a year plus public holidays. French workers have a total of forty leave days a year, Austrians thirty-eight, and Germans, thirty-four.[1]

Another policy is maternity leave—how much paid leave does a new mother receive? The U.S. Family and Medical Leave Act requires that public agencies and private employers with more than fifty employees provide up to a total of twelve work-weeks of unpaid leave.[2] Again, many other countries do much better: France provides sixteen weeks, and the U.K., thirty-nine.[3] Another critical change for families would be more flexible work hours and schedules for working parents. Working more from home and more leeway in office hours helps in accommodating the needs of children and busy family scheduling.

These kinds of family-investment public and corporate policies can be of great significance for a struggling family, providing time for important and family-friendly rest and relaxation, as well as support for critical life passages like having a new child. We all know the importance of time with family, and both business and public policy could do much more to support that valuable principle.

LIFE LESSONS FROM THE LITTLE LEAGUE PLAYING FIELD

Little League parents often tease me that the things I constantly tell the kids from the sidelines are really "lessons for life." For example, you can hear me calling out things like: "Pretend the ball is coming to you!" "Know what you're going to do before the play begins!" "Get ready for every pitch, even if you don't swing!" "Run out every hit!" Or my favorite, "Look alive out there!"

We have developed three goals for our baseball teams: first, to have fun; second, to be good teammates (if we have an ironclad rule on our team, it is this: no negative talk, especially when someone makes a mistake, because we all make mistakes—even the coaches); and third, to learn and love the game of baseball. Later in life, kids will less likely remember the scores or the standings from their Little League years than they will the kind of experience it was for them. Although some of my players (my son for one) dream of a Major League Baseball career, that is unlikely. But the lessons they learn as Little Leaguers will stay with them for a lifetime.

One of the most important things Little League can teach kids is to separate achievement and love. When my cleanup batter Luke powers one of his monster hits over the centerfielder's head to win a playoff game, he can feel his coach's delight and pride. But when he goes for a too-high pitch and strikes out with guys on base, he needs to never doubt his dad's love and support.

> ONE OF THE MOST IMPORTANT THINGS LITTLE LEAGUE CAN TEACH KIDS IS TO SEPARATE ACHIEVEMENT AND LOVE.

In our league championship game, there was an incident that reminded me why I coach Little League. We were up 3–2 in the top of the sixth inning. The other team got a runner to second with one out. On the next play, a ground ball skidded to our third baseman, Timmy, who missed it, leaving the tying run safe at third. You could hear a collective gasp from the crowd and see how crushed Timmy felt. On the next play, a pop fly went to the same kid! He dropped it, and their runner dashed home to tie the game. This time the nine-year-old was devastated and began to cry.

I called time and went over to third. The sobbing little boy pleaded with me to take him out of the game. "Let me just sit on the bench, coach. I can't play anymore!" I told him to take a deep breath and to look at me. "Timmy," I said, "you're here because I believe in you. I am not taking you out of the game. You're a good ball player, Timmy, and all good players sometimes drop the ball. I need you right here on third base. Just remember, your next play is much more important than your last play. You can do this."

I could feel how upset the boy was, and I could sense his parents' pain from the sidelines, knowing that an experience like this could leave a long-lasting impression. The umpire yelled, "Play ball." We got another out. Unbelievably, another fly ball soared up over third base. I heard a voice, small but with authority, cry out, "I got it!" And Timmy did. End of inning. And, in our last bat, we scored the winning run, on a dramatic steal of home, to win the league championship. Afterward, I gathered all the boys on the grass and said to them, "First, one of us had a tough moment . . . and then made the game-winning catch. Let's hear it for Timmy!" The cheers went up for the kid who needed a second (or third) chance to succeed. And later, Timmy was the first to get his trophy. His parents e-mailed me the next week to happily tell me that their son had already signed up for the next season's baseball.

SPIRITUAL DISCIPLINES AND BEDTIME PRAYERS

Becoming a father rather late in life has indeed taught me many things. In fact, many of life's most important lessons, I would have to say, have come to me by way of finally being a dad. These two boys have become a spiritual anchor for me, and being their dad has been a contemplative discipline that my busy life sorely needs. I began to build my speaking and travel schedule around things like Little League baseball, or even just putting them to bed at night—which I now do most nights. After a while, I realized I wasn't just doing this for them—but also for me. I simply can't bear not hearing the daily reports about what happened at school or after school or with their friends. And their prayers before going to bed at night (my job) are surely not to be missed. They now help shape my theology.

Jack's latest pearl was praying for his mom and dad and brother and cousins and classmates—as usual. Then he and his brother often pray for "poor people," but this time Jack added, "And, God, there are a lot of poor people, hungry people, and homeless people—any comments or questions? . . . Amen." Jack is used to an interactive classroom and wanted to know what God thought about there being so many poor people out there!

> BEING THEIR DAD HAS BEEN A CONTEMPLATIVE DISCIPLINE THAT MY BUSY LIFE SORELY NEEDS.

A few months ago, I could tell that Luke was trying to work out, in his prayer life, what he had heard about almost thirty thousand children dying every day around the world due to hunger and disease. He said, "Dear God, I pray that all those children won't die again tomorrow . . . (sigh) but that's unlikely. So, dear God, I pray . . . that it will be their best day ever . . . but that's stupid. So, dear God . . . help us to stop this from happening." Sitting there in the dark, with tears running down my face, I could only offer a quiet amen. How could I miss those prayers?

I once coined a phrase that entered Washington parlance among some political and media pundits: "A budget is a moral document." But being a dad to Luke and Jack, I now have a new phrase: "A calendar is a moral document."

And it's all about the calendar. I used to say that a budget tells you what and who are most important to a family, church, city, state, or nation. And that's certainly also true about a calendar. It tells us who or what is most important to us.

Thomas Merton once said, "In the end, it is the reality of personal relationships that saves everything."[4] And for me, the greatest blessings are clearly to be a family with Joy, Luke, and Jack; to enjoy an extended family of brothers and sisters, nieces and nephews, who still are very conscious of the legacy of love that our now departed parents left us. Add to that some of the best friends and companions anyone could be blessed to have and the opportunity to regularly meet people on the road who express a deep solidarity and kindred spirit with us in this emerging movement that marries faith and justice—especially a new generation. These are the things that give me hope.

> I NOW HAVE A NEW PHRASE: "A CALENDAR IS A MORAL DOCUMENT."

13

THE MEANING OF
WORK AND THE
ETHIC OF SERVICE

Jobs have been a central focus of this economic recession, and the unemployment rate a consistent measure of how we are doing. Losing homes and jobs are two of the most personal economic losses people experience. And for decades now, before this recession, the wages of low- and even middle-income families have stagnated, even while the income of those at the top of the economic pyramid has skyrocketed. The loss of benefits has paralleled the decline in real wages.

While we need jobs to come back, wages to go up, and benefits to be restored, I would suggest that we need more. I believe we need to focus on the quality of *work* as well as the quantity of *jobs*. We need to talk not just about occupation, but vocation. Not just about what fills up our time, but about the things that make our time meaningful. This recession offers us the opportunity to look at that deeper question: work as well as jobs. People need good jobs, but people also need good work.

A NEW DEFINITION OF *WORK*

In our many faith traditions, work is central. We speak of "God's work" and the need to make that our own. Our greatest religious traditions all teach us that God works. As beings created in his image, we reflect not only God's capacity for work, but that work is a primary part of our identity and our reflection of God's image. The work of our hands is one way of offering worship back to God. And, indeed, we are to see ourselves as co-workers with God, helping to accomplish the purposes of God in the world.

> PEOPLE NEED GOOD JOBS, BUT PEOPLE ALSO NEED GOOD WORK.

But too often, and for far too many people, the problems with work go beyond the lack of good wages and benefits; they include a lack of purpose and meaning in work. And it is time to remember that purpose and meaning in work are also important, alongside pay and perks. They are not luxuries, as some economic realists might suggest, but part of the intended nature of work as our service to God and his creation. Our work is a critical component of being good stewards of God's creation and part of our service to our neighbors. Our work, in other words, is intended to be good for creation, for our neighbors, and for ourselves.

Again, the opportunity this crisis offers us is the chance to rethink the important question of work. Before the economic crisis, many of us in secure jobs sometimes looked down on those who were not working as simply lazy. While there is always a segment of the population that does not want to work, this new economic downturn has exposed the myth of a welfare class unwilling to work, as many hard-working, industrious people now find themselves without jobs.

But we need to start talking more about the meaning of our work and not just the money we get from it. A challenge for societies throughout history has been determining ways that all people are able to participate in work that promotes human dignity and respect. In the Hebrew Bible, we read the story of Ruth, who was able to be a creative participant in the economy because of the laws concerning gleaning, a kind of subsidized work. The prophet Isaiah's vision of a good society included that the people "shall long enjoy the work of their hands. They shall not labor in vain." [1] And one of the psalms of blessing includes the promise that "You shall eat the fruit of the labor of your hands; you shall be happy, and it shall go well with you." [2]

Stephen Smith is a Harvard graduate with a master's degree from the London School of Economics and is now the chief operating officer of a bakery that employs formerly homeless people and those with disabilities. He is married to Sara Whitaker, a first-generation college graduate and Northwestern law student, who started a nonprofit in her spare time to help young high-school women become first-generation college students. Stephen and Sara represent a new generation of young people, and many others of all ages, who believe that their work counts for more than just a paycheck.

> WE NEED TO START TALKING MORE ABOUT THE MEANING OF OUR WORK AND NOT JUST THE MONEY WE GET FROM IT.

The book *Shop Class as Soulcraft* tells the story of a young man with a PhD in political philosophy who realizes that his passion does not lie in an office job writing papers, but in motorcycle repair. We should never diminish the importance of higher education, but we have placed too great an emphasis on a very narrow form of work and have disregarded the importance and challenge of work with our hands. *Fight Club, Office Space,* and the American and British versions of *The Office* have been great hits because they speak to an underlying truth: we aren't all cut from the same cloth, and cubicle work isn't always fulfilling. One of the fasting growing internships in the summer of 2009 involved students working on organic or family farms.

Most people yearn for more creativity in their work lives, and this crisis could be a springboard for reigniting our creative spark. We now have the opportunity to place a new focus on vocation, and even "calling," in the workplace. Rabbi Jonathan Sacks says it well in *The Dignity of Difference*: "Work has a spiritual value, labor elevates man, for by it he earns his food. What concerned the rabbis was the self respect that came from work as against unearned income. . . . Animals find sustenance; only man creates it.[3]

SLINGING CRACK-ROCK

In 2000, right before tech stocks tanked, a movie called *The Boiler Room* opened with a telling monologue from the movie's main character, Seth Davis.

I read this article a while back that said that Microsoft employs more millionaire secretaries than any other company in the world. They took stock options over Christmas bonuses. It was a good move. I remember there was this picture, of one of the groundskeepers next to his Ferrari. Blew my mind. You see s*** like that, and it just plants seeds, makes you think it's possible, even easy. And then you turn on the TV, and there's just more of it. The $87 million lottery winner, that kid actor that just made $20 million on his last movie, that internet stock that shot through the roof, you could have made millions if you had just gotten in early, and that's exactly what I wanted to do: get in. I didn't want to be an innovator any more, I just wanted to make the quick and easy buck, I just wanted in. The Notorious BIG said it best: "Either you're slingin' crack-rock, or you've got a wicked jump-shot." Nobody wants to work for it anymore. There's no honor in taking that after school job at Mickey Dee's; honor's in the dollar, kid. So I went the white boy way of slinging crack-rock: I became a stock broker.

For years, this statement seemed to pretty well define the thoughts and hopes of some of America's best and brightest minds. A survey of the men in the Harvard class of 2007 who went directly to jobs found that "more than 58 percent opted for careers in finance or consulting, with fully 20 percent going into investment banking, the most lucrative specialty of all."[4]

Adam Smith shares a disturbing but frighteningly honest assessment of our society's heroes: "The disposition to admire, and almost to worship, the rich and the powerful, and to despise, or, at least, to neglect persons of poor and mean condition is the great and most universal cause of the corruption of our moral sentiments."[5]

While the percentage of those living in extreme poverty has continued to decline, we are still confronted with the fact that three billion people (virtually half of God's children on the planet) still live on less than two dollars a day, and that is the principal *moral reality* of today's global economy. The corruption of our "moral sentiments" is the reason that fact is seldom mentioned in our conversations about the market. But if we are to

> WE ARE STILL CONFRONTED WITH THE FACT THAT THREE BILLION PEOPLE (VIRTUALLY HALF OF GOD'S CHILDREN ON THE PLANET) STILL LIVE ON LESS THAN TWO DOLLARS A DAY.

recover our moral sentiments, that reality must supersede all others and be the defining fact that shapes our moral recovery from this economic recession.

SERVICE AS VOCATION

But here's some good news. In summer 2009, I had a visit from Wendy Kopp, the founder of Teach For America. This rapidly growing program invites the best and the brightest of our college graduates to come to the toughest neighborhoods in America, walk into the worst schools in the country, and work with the poorest and most undereducated students in the nation. What an opportunity! But I learned from Wendy that Teach For America accepted just 15 percent of its record thirty-five thousand applications last year; the program that sends some of the most talented college graduates into the nation's most hopeless schools is now harder to get into than most Ivy League universities.

Those two avenues now define the moral landscape for a new generation of young people in America: the desire to be investment bankers or the desire to Teach For America. The cultural message that the measure of success, and of life, is wealth—as much as you can get—has been literally screaming at them. At the same time, a new message is emerging: that service to your neighbor and the common good is more rewarding and fulfilling than the endless pursuit of individual gain. The call to service has been growing, even before the Great Recession, but may now be one of the most important shifts to come out of this crisis.

AmeriCorps and Peace Corps are also growing quickly; and a myriad of faith-based organizations are attracting the best of a younger generation of believers into years of internships that take them into the poorest and toughest American hoods and the most impoverished slums of the developing world. I love the motto of one of those organizations, the Jesuit Volunteer Corps: "Ruined for Life." That is indeed the *purpose* of the best programs; to change the trajectory of a life and to make that volunteer into a different kind of future teacher, doctor, nurse, lawyer, community organizer, business entrepreneur, artist, architect, technician, scientist, minister, or whatever else he or she will eventually become; and also a different kind of parent, parishioner, and citizen.

> A NEW MESSAGE IS EMERGING: THAT SERVICE TO YOUR NEIGHBOR AND THE COMMON GOOD IS MORE REWARDING AND FULFILLING THAN THE ENDLESS PURSUIT OF INDIVIDUAL GAIN.

While volunteer service is, of course, voluntary, good public policy can encourage people to serve and help enable them to do so. Many high schools now require a certain number of community-service hours to graduate, and many public-school systems sponsor mentoring and tutoring programs. In the spring of 2009, Congress took a major step by passing the Edward M. Kennedy Serve America Act. The Serve America Act reauthorized and expanded the Corporation for National and Community Service, a federal agency created in 1993. "The corporation involves four million Americans in result-driven service each year, including 75,000 AmeriCorps members, 492,000 Senior Corps volunteers, 1.1 million Learn and Serve America students, and 2.2 million additional community volunteers." The act will enable both expanding these programs and initiating new ones.[6]

This new generation is the most civically engaged and service oriented since the generations that came of age during the Great Depression and the social movements of the 1960s. New waves of volunteers are flooding nonprofits with energy, commitment, and ideas. And many are thinking more about their vocations than their careers, more about their gifts than their assets, and more about their calling than their niche in the market.

COMMON-GOOD CULTURE

The greed culture is not just wrong; it has failed, and it is time to replace it with a common-good culture. But a common-good culture must be built, not just wished for, by creating new economic and civic institutions that lead the country to new/old values by example. We must both build new models of "social capitalism"—as Nobel Peace Prize winner Muhammad Yunus envisions—and more dynamic organizations in the not-for-profit world, which are aimed more at making social change than providing social services. What are often called charitable organizations or nonprofits must move beyond simply meeting existing needs to also taking on some of our greatest challenges—as organizations like Teach For America are trying to do.

> THIS NEW GENERATION IS THE MOST CIVICALLY ENGAGED AND SERVICE ORIENTED SINCE THE GENERATIONS THAT CAME OF AGE DURING THE GREAT DEPRESSION AND THE SOCIAL MOVEMENTS OF THE 1960S.

We can't change the whole world, the country, or even a local community all at once; but we can claim the old idea of the "parish." That means to take responsibility for where you live, work, learn, or worship—a neighborhood or a community for which we are challenged to help grow, transform, and build a better quality of life.

The idea of a strong civil society is not liberal or conservative—it is radical. The decline of our civic sector is at the very root of our economic crisis, and our challenge to rebuild it will be at the heart of a sustained recovery. It is in the voluntary institutions where we most build social capital, create trust, develop community, and strengthen the moral fabric of our society. The success and the health of both the market and the state are dependent upon the values, virtues, and commitments that are best grown in this "third sector."

Churches can play a key leadership role here, as the most prevalent institutions in any community. Perhaps it is time to create a whole new adult Sunday-school curriculum on biblical economics and moral recovery and about the religious call to social service and social justice. The gospel story of the feeding of the five thousand can be a modern parable teaching that when each of us shares our "loaves and fishes," they tend to multiply. New social patterns of mutual aid and cooperative solutions to the problems of credit, jobs, housing, health care, and energy transformation can be piloted at the local level, then scaled up. A burst of creativity would be the best response to an economic recession.

> THE IDEA OF A STRONG CIVIL SOCIETY IS NOT LIBERAL OR CONSERVATIVE; IT IS RADICAL.

A NEW SOCIAL COVENANT

We fundamentally need to find a way to create a new social contract, even a social covenant. Contracts are agreements between parties and dictate transfers of wealth or power, but covenants are deeper and more fundamental: they define relationships. The U.S. Declaration of Independence was a covenant that declared a new relationship between the people of this country and mother England, but also among themselves. It also declared the guiding values and principles for a new nation. Our Constitution is more of a contract that defines legal obligations. But the contract of the Constitution, without the covenant of the Declaration, would have seemed incomplete, and even hollow.

Service is becoming a valued societal activity and a way to bring us together. We are slowly becoming a service nation. The next move would be to become an "opportunity nation," whose values affirm practices and policies that would help lift millions of our citizens and neighbors around the world out of poverty. A commitment to overcome poverty in the world's wealthiest nation, along with new solutions to global poverty, could easily become the social movement of our time, a new "altar call" for a new generation of those who call themselves spiritual but not necessarily religious. And it would be nothing less than a new *conversion*.

PART SIX

RECOVERING "THE COMMONS"

14

REGAINING
OUR BALANCE

As every one of our kids who has taken basic American history or civics knows, our government is built on the principle of checks and balances. Each branch of government is intended to serve its own purpose and help ensure that the others do the same. When all of them are functioning well, they should support and even challenge the others. Of course, it doesn't always work perfectly, or even well, but the principle is always invoked when things get out of kilter, and the argument is made that we need to restore the proper "balance."

Our society is the same way. We have the *public sector* (the state), the *private sector* (the market), and the *civic sector* (our voluntary and nonprofit institutions—including the faith community). When any one of those begins to take over the others, or one is weakened and does not perform its functions, all sectors are in trouble—and so are we. Is there any doubt that we have lost that balance and that the critical cross-sector roles have been eclipsed in the last few decades by the almost total dominance of the market? The important checks of market excesses that the public sector is supposed to provide had mostly disappeared; and the tempering of the market's desires and agendas by the voice of civil society institutions had been weakened or even muted.

The Great Recession has revealed great imbalances in our society, and in fact, the crisis has been largely caused by them. Some have likened the picture of the three sectors to the metaphor of a three-legged stool. What we have seen is how the market leg of the stool has grown enormously, and the dominance of the market over all else has caused our society to literally fall over. The economy itself began to crumble like the famous house of cards. The public sector has not played its necessary role for the past three decades, and the civic sector has been forced to clean up the mess of the consequences of the great imbalance.

Personal and social irresponsibility in the private (or market) sector has been an enormous contributing factor to this crisis. The current crisis was created by decades of social deregulation, allowing major corporations and banks to engage in what I will call "short-term selfishness," which ultimately compromises not only the common good but their own good in the long term. And the cultural consequences in the erosion of good values, as we have seen, has compromised our moral integrity as a society and threatened our most precious things, including the future of our children. We have gone through a period of failure—failure to teach, encourage, expect, and re-enforce both personal *and* social responsibility. Therefore, our postcrisis period will require a whole new ethic and expecta-

> THE GREAT RECESSION HAS REVEALED GREAT IMBALANCES IN OUR SOCIETY, AND IN FACT, THE CRISIS HAS BEEN PARTLY CAUSED BY THEM.

tion of different personal and social behavior from business, civil society, and public governance. Indeed, that is a great redemptive promise of this crisis.

A new ethic of social responsibility will require a framework of new social regulation in which critical entrepreneurial activity can best take place. And, at a very deep level, we must decide that *budgets, too, are moral documents*, reflecting what and who we think are important. But this crisis is both structural and spiritual. And while new regulation and responsibility by our government is vitally necessary, it will be woefully inadequate without new self-regulation and responsibility from both employers and employees, civic leaders and government officials, parents and children.

This chapter will explore how to rebalance the three-legged stool, which has fallen over, and how to restore the proper place of the market, the necessary role of government, and the creative contribution of the nonprofit sector.

THE STRENGTH OF THE COMMONS

It might just be an urban legend told by tour guides, but I have heard that to this day, it is perfectly legal for Boston residents to bring their cows to graze in the Boston Commons. *The Commons* is an old-fashioned term that we do not hear much anymore. Since medieval times and right through the founding of Boston, it was a regular practice that certain land would be set aside for common use. Any resident, rich or poor, could bring livestock to the commons to graze or feed. It was a policy in agrarian societies that fought directly against inequality by allowing every community member to have the resources needed to raise up at least some livestock and other farm animals.

In his 1968 essay, "The Tragedy of the Commons," Garrett Hardin described some of the reasons why these commons would sometimes be overgrazed and collapse. As community members would bring their livestock to graze, each one would have an interest in seeing his animals eat their fill and stay healthy. It is, of course, in the interest of community members to see the commons stay healthy so that they can continue to bring their livestock back year after year. But since every community member has a strong interest in seeing his livestock healthy *this year*, and not a strong interest in seeing the commons healthy five or ten years down the line, the commons would often end up depleted.

Today, the Commons of our society are not represented primarily by areas for our livestock to graze. Rather, they are the fresh water we drink and the air we breathe. There are those who have advocated that we should privatize and sell all of our water and air. They argue that it is only through the private ownership of all of the Commons that the proper incentives will remain in place to preserve them in the long term. It is through abolishing these remaining limits on the market, and its expansion to all of our natural resources, that they will, in fact, be redeemed.

> HISTORY HAS SHOWN THAT PRIVATE ENTERPRISE HAS NOT BEEN OUR BEST ADVOCATE FOR PRESERVING THESE NATURAL RESOURCES.

But history has shown that private enterprise has not been our best advocate for preserving these natural resources. In fact, private enterprise, without regulation, hastens the use of our natural resources. The collective drive of communities for long-term preservation is much stronger than the individual drive concerned primarily with profit. The other response to protect the Commons is not to sell them but to form a social contract, and to voluntarily and democratically regulate their use.

Instead of trusting the "invisible hand," we must be more honest about the human tendency to think in the short term and to overuse our resources, and we need to regulate accordingly. It is through the democratic process that we are able to hold ourselves and our businesses accountable to a longer-term vision for where we want to be as a country and how we want to use the good gifts that God has given. The decisions that elected officials make and the priorities we promote through the democratic process may either slow down or speed up the rate of economic growth. They are also able to affect how much time we spend with our families, the gap between rich and poor, and the preservation of our natural resources. It very well might be possible to hasten the growth of our GDP if we give no consideration to these things, but our system of government allows us to also make other priorities important, not just raw economic growth.

THE MYTH OF THE SINLESS MARKET

Rebecca Blank, a labor economist at the Brookings Institution and long-time leader in the United Church of Christ, has articulated the intersection between her faith as a Christian and her work as an economist. It is her faith that has helped her realize the importance of her work in building models to understand our market economy, but it has also revealed the limitations of those models for understanding the market and the world. She says, "To use religious language, there is sin in the world. And sometimes people do things that are, in the long run, quite harmful to themselves, as well as others, for the sake of short-term greed."[1]

There is a common fallacy in the way people and politicians often think of the market. Serious economists from Adam Smith to John Maynard Keynes and even Milton Friedman understood and articulated that the market has limits. Friedman once said,

> "SOMETIMES PEOPLE DO THINGS THAT ARE, IN THE LONG RUN, QUITE HARMFUL, FOR THE SAKE OF SHORT-TERM GREED."

"I would like to be a zero-government libertarian, [but] I don't think it's a feasible social structure. I look over history, and outside of perhaps Iceland, where else can you find any historical examples of that kind of a system developing?"[2] And now, even Iceland, the best example of a limited government state in the world, became so off balance that, in October 2008, it became the only industrialized nation to ever need a bailout from the International Monetary Fund.

To hear some zealots of the free market talk, you would think they believe in a sinless market, where no regulations are allowed, no limitations accepted, no restraints needed, and no accountability required. In other words, the market is beyond sin and shortcomings. The logic goes that, left to its own devices, the market will behave in a perfect or sinless fashion and, in fact, only it can provide the moral framework in which everything else should operate.

In light of the Great Recession, can we still hold on to that bad theology? It's not just liberals who cannot accept this bad theology of economics, but true conservatives shouldn't either. As Rebecca Blank points out, we do not live in a sinless world, markets included, and some limits, restraints, accountabilities, and checks and balances are both morally and practically required. To believe in a market that does not need outside regulation, a market that is wholly capable of regulating itself, is to believe in essence, in a market that is not subject to human fallibility, folly, and, yes, sin. As we already examined, it is a tempting belief but an idolatrous one, and it projects a quality that only belongs to God onto a tower made by humankind. Yet, the myth of the sinless market persists.

The I'll Be Gone mentality discussed earlier in this book should not surprise us. What every parent hopes to teach his or her children, and a quality that is often quite difficult to model, is the ability to delay gratification. Without discipline, we all have the tendency to accept short-term gratification without considering the consequences down the road. This was certainly true in the financial industry in the run-up to the Great Recession. Bankers and investors engaged in deals that were immediately lucrative and profitable without full consideration of the long-term consequences. In fact, many of those who did not engage in those risky practices were left behind and experienced losses because they couldn't keep up.

In the midst of our housing boom, some banks began to offer mortgages without requiring people to prove assets. Others soon followed suit. In the race to the bottom, banks began to offer mortgages even without proof of income. Still others soon followed suit. Those who engaged in these practices experienced enormous short-term gains. Just think of the huge compensation package the CEO of Countrywide Financial was receiving just a few short years ago. Eventually, the market crash revealed this mistake at the cost of millions of Americans losing their homes. The ripple effects have been so great that both the responsible and irresponsible are feeling the repercussions. This book is not a treatise on the best financial regulations for banks or hedge funds, but a call that our country engage in serious discussions about what regulations or transparency requirements might help mitigate this type of race to the bottom for short-term profits in the future.

The market is not designed to regulate itself or rid itself from "sin." Excesses are inevitable and can only be curbed by values and forces that come from outside the market. Robert Reich in his book *Supercapitalism* put it this way: "Corporate Executives are not authorized by anyone—least of all by their consumers or investors—to balance profits against the public good. Nor do they have any expertise in making such moral calculations. That's why we live in a democracy, in which government is supposed to represent the public in drawing such lines."[3]

RACE TO THE TOP

Corporate executives are legally bound to the interests of their shareholders. Long-term business sense and good corporate ethics will go a long way, but they won't solve the problem entirely. What happens when a small business owner who sacrifices his own share of profits to ensure a good wage and health benefits for his workers is faced with a corporate giant who hires at slashed wages and offers no benefits? That business owner will have to race to the bottom to try and maintain profitability. He will have to sacrifice his consideration for what is right in order to stay profitable. But we as a society can democratically decide what base wages should be, or that health insurance is provided to all, or that retirement benefits are in place. Then that same business owner is free to run his business both by what is right and what is profitable.

> WE AS A SOCIETY CAN DEMOCRATICALLY DECIDE WHAT BASE WAGES SHOULD BE, OR THAT HEALTH INSURANCE IS PROVIDED TO ALL, OR THAT RETIREMENT BENEFITS ARE IN PLACE.

Raising the minimum wage has been a contentious issue as businesses are concerned that it will hurt their profits and end up having the unintended effect of increasing labor costs and forcing layoffs. But many states that have raised the minimum wage above the federal level have found this not to be the case. For example, Washington, which indexes the minimum wage to inflation each year, has the highest minimum wage and a strong economy.[4] When people at the low end of the income spectrum get raises, all of that money goes right back into the economy as they buy basic necessities and consumer goods. More money at the bottom means more money being spent at businesses, which is a great way to stimulate an economy.

While Milton Friedman and I would not have agreed on social-programs policy or even the minimum wage, he recognized that money in the hands of poor people is a good way to increase consumer spending. He promoted a minimum income for poor people in the country to do exactly that. It was this theory that paved the way for the passing of the Earned Income Tax Credit as a policy for increasing overall income for the working poor in our country—a very successful public-policy commitment that has broad bipartisan support.

As the CEO of a nonprofit, I am keenly aware of the huge costs that benefits like health care incurs for any small operation and the extremely limited choices we have to address those costs. Deciding to cover health-care costs for all our employees and their families has been a costly commitment for Sojourners but one we thought necessary to lead by example. But costs like these also make it much more difficult for small businesses and even large corporations to compete globally with businesses in other countries that do not have to shoulder these costs themselves.

Removing the bulk of health-care

> REMOVING THE BULK OF HEALTH-CARE COSTS FROM LABOR COSTS IN OUR COUNTRY COULD GREATLY INCREASE THE COMPETIVENESS OF OUR BUSINESSES.

costs from labor costs in our country could greatly increase the competiveness of our businesses. Guaranteeing individuals access to affordable quality coverage will also help the flexibility of our workforce. People often stay in jobs they do not like or find fulfilling because they are concerned they will lose coverage or have a gap in coverage that could cause problems later on. Security in knowing that you won't go bankrupt because you might get sick would free up more of our country's entrepreneurs and innovators to do what they do best—strike out and start something new.

A NEW EQUILIBRIUM

Freedom from undue restrictions is a necessary part of human flourishing, but so too, as our religious traditions teach us, is sometimes submitting to limitations. In a market economy, too much regulation can indeed stifle innovation and have unintended consequences, but every day there are regulators silently at work keeping our children's toys free of toxins, making our cars safe, and our food fresh. Do we really want them all to stop their work? In the name of not wanting small business to suffer from too many overburdening regulations, we have dropped the blanket of deregulation over the behavior of our largest corporations and the financial giants of Wall Street—and that has proven to have been a colossal mistake. The issue of scale could become a key metric for social regulation and even moral accountability. Smaller and newer enterprises may need more room to operate and fewer regulatory burdens to bear; while the largest corporations are held much more accountable to the regulations that preserve the common good—because they have such a huge impact on it. When some businesses have become "too big to fail," perhaps they have just become too big. Markets will always have ups and downs, and we cannot wish that away, but these downturns also test our character as a community and as a country.

It is of the utmost importance for economists to keep in mind that while their work is focused on the functioning of our economy, our economy is not the only measure of how we judge our society in moral and human terms. Blank says, "I think that the true moral question that faces society is when we go into the downturn, how do we respond to the people who are hurt? What do we have in place that helps those who lose their houses and pension savings, who find themselves struggling and in pain?"

The moral compass must be about real people and their real lives. Indeed, it is our connections to our neighbors that help us achieve this social balance. And without some humility, ideologies run away with themselves and become self-consuming. The key principle that helps us discern the right path is always *balance*. In the 1930s, socialist and communist political parties sprang up in our country and advocated for nationalizing all major industries, uprooting the private market, and doing away with wage systems. Today, the only socialist in Congress, Senator Bernie Sanders, would not even agree to that. The battle has been fought and won, the argument has been made and triumphed, that government cannot and should not be the central system for running our economy. That sort of system creates a devastating imbalance. But the real battle now is not capitalism versus socialism, but the unrestrained market versus genuine democracy. We have seen the tyranny of the all-powerful market; and it is time to reassert our best and most basic traditions of democratic accountability.

We must find a new sort of equilibrium. More and more people feel as if the companies they work for or the stores they shop at are not responsive to them. Small business owners are beholden to the ebb and flow of global business cycles far beyond their control. Families and communities feel that their lives are lived at the behest of the market, instead of the market serving them. The same frustration is also true of our relationship to government. More and more elections feel like reality TV— professionally produced infomercials whose outcome has already been determined.

These feelings of helplessness and powerlessness in regard to both our government and our economy have also come about, in part, because we have neglected the strength and importance of the third leg of our stool. The third leg is made up of our churches, our mosques, and synagogues. It is comprised of all of our voluntary associations, clubs, and organizations where we come together with others to discuss and focus on the common good. It is in these places that we work with one another to accomplish shared goals and ends. This could mean volunteering more of our time and resources to help those around us; it could mean using our collective voice to influence the government or our buying power to influence businesses. The invigoration of the civil society sector is a crucial and necessary part of our recovery.

One of the important roles that the faith community can play, indeed any person who cares about the character of our country can play, is a *prophetic role*. Blank describes it as "going to policy makers and saying, you cannot cut these programs, you have to respond to this pain—saying, 'We as a community of faith care about the widows and orphans, those who are homeless and marginalized . . . and we demand that the institutions within our civic society respond as well.' It is very important for congregations to keep articulating a sense of priorities about what it is that government needs to be doing in a recession to provide the safety net and help those who are hurting."

REORDERING

Humility, balance, priorities, and limits. These are the discussions that the faith community must and should be having with some of the most powerful economic and political leaders of our time. Ethics and values should not be seen in competition to good business and well-functioning markets, but as a necessary component of and sometimes crucial counterpoint to them. Ethical ideas must be held accountable to practical outcomes, and those concerned with bottom lines must be challenged by their moral responsibility to all of God's children.

We need nothing less than social transformation to come out of this Great Recession, and it is my hope that this change could also represent a transformation of the role of government. This doesn't mean an abolition of government nor should it represent a takeover. Instead, it could represent a proactive and democratically responsive government that is a partner with private enterprise and not a competitor or controller over it.

Sin can be described as a kind of disordering. Everything God created has a specific purpose, use, and order. Sin enters the picture when humans lose that purpose, when they misuse what God has created and disorder the world around us. This disorder or sin is quite clear in the world and in our economy today. Because we are sinful, we do not always act in accordance with our own interests or the interests of others. It is naive to assume otherwise, and the Bible is quite clear that government has a positive role in both preserving order and promoting good for the society.

St. Paul said, "Rulers are not a terror to good conduct, but to bad. Do you wish to have no fear of the authority? Then do what is good, and you will receive its approval, for it is God's servant for your good. But if you do what is wrong, you should be afraid, for the authority does not bear the sword in vain! It is the servant of God to execute wrath on the wrongdoer."[5] In this passage, Paul argues that it is the proper role of government to punish bad conduct and also to act as God's servant for our good. These are two things that a well-functioning government can and should do.

Christians who lived under the Roman Empire were also fully aware of the abuse of government powers, as many Christians died as martyrs at the hand of the state. In Revelation 13, St. John wrote about the Roman Empire as a sort of demonic force used as a tool of the devil. When John wrote the book of Revelation as a letter to early Christian congregations, he was in exile on the island of Patmos, in trouble for preaching the gospel. He had good reason to be upset! As someone who has been arrested over twenty times in nonviolent protests of government policies, I, too, am one who certainly believes that government is not always good.

While our country continues to wrestle with many of these questions in pursuit of a "more perfect union," we are able to see other countries, and American businesses in those countries, wrestle with them as well. Robert Reich tells a story of Yahoo in China that gave me pause. In 2005, Yahoo handed over to the Chinese government the names of Chinese dissidents who used Yahoo e-mail accounts to try and hide their identities. As a result, one reporter was sentenced to ten years in prison for sending to foreigners a message he had received from Chinese authorities telling their newspaper to downplay the fifteenth anniversary of the Tiananmen Square massacre. Yahoo defended its actions by saying that they had to play by China's rules in order to continue their presence in the country and provide the long-term good of opening the country to Western influences.

In an interesting piece of what I would consider moral theology, a Chinese dissident named Liu Xiaobo, who had spent time in a Chinese prison himself, saw it differently. In an open letter to Yahoo's founder, Jerry Yang, he wrote, "I must tell you that my indignation at and contempt for you and your company are not a bit less than my indignation at and contempt for the communist regime. . . . Profit makes you dull in morality. Did it ever occur to you that it is a shame for you to be considered a traitor to your customer? . . . [Y]our glorious social status is a poor cover for your barren morality, and your swelling wallet is an indicator of your diminished status as a man."[6]

We have the privilege and freedom—no, the responsibility—in a constitutional democracy, to challenge and shape our government. It is for this reason that I have both pride in and hope for our country. We must always hold in tension that government can be a servant for good or the perpetuator of great evil. Just as there is the danger of the market's becoming God, so, too, is there the danger of the state becoming God. Both are idolatry.

The new conversation should be about balance, not the endless ideological debates between socialism and capitalism. We need to regain the notion of *roles* and *limits* to the various sectors of society and a new era of public/private solutions to many of our social problems.

15

THE PARABLE OF
DETROIT AND THE
GREEN SHOOTS
OF HOPE

Recently, I was speaking and visiting in my old hometown, accompanied by my twenty-four-year-old special assistant, Tim King. Tim was shocked and quite shaken by the pain and suffering of Detroit—parts of which now look like the worst places in the Third World. The *depression* has already come to Detroit, and it is a brutal picture of the nation we could become if the economic *recession* were to get even worse. But Tim was even more shocked when I told him what it was like growing up in Detroit's good old days during the 1950s and '60s.

My dad worked for Detroit Edison, the area's power utility. And almost all my friend's dads worked for Ford, General Motors, Chrysler, or Edison. They were all returning veterans from World War II and all had jobs that could support a family on one income, with health insurance and other benefits. We all lived in three-bedroom houses financed by the newly created Federal Housing Insurance Corporation—a government program aimed at helping returning servicemen get into their first homes. We were a city of homeowners. We kids all went to good and safe public schools, we all knew we could get jobs where our dads worked if we wanted to, and we were all hopeful for the future. Detroit was the fourth largest city in the United States—and we all knew that was right behind New York, Chicago, and Los Angeles! My dad used to tell his five kids, "We live in the best city, in the best country, in the whole world!" The engines of Detroit's automobiles were purring, and nobody ever expected our one-industry town to "run out of gas," as *Time* magazine recently put it.

But it wasn't so wonderful for Detroit's black community, of course, which I discovered as a teenager, learning that there were really two cities maybe working side by side, but living quite separately, in the Motor City. And in 1967 the rest of the nation discovered how separate we truly were when the Detroit riots rocked the country; revealing the strict segregation of our neighborhoods and schools, the deep economic and educational disparities, the quite brutal behavior of the city's almost all-white police force (creating the incident that sparked the riot), with an almost total blindness in the white community to the invisible walls of Detroit's institutional racism. After the riots, the "white flight" to the suburbs which was already occurring then accelerated, soon creating a majority black city entrenched in the politics of racial division, fueled by too many leaders on both sides of the color line.

My parents helped to start the little church that became our family's virtual second home. My father was a mechanical engineer by training and a rising young executive at Edison, but his real love was his role as a lay pastor at Dunning Park Chapel, in Redford Township, an "assembly" in the evangelical Plymouth

Brethren tradition. There, for Sunday services (mornings and evenings), Wednesday night prayer meetings, ladies' meetings, men's meetings, elders' meetings, youth activities, and often more, the workers from the big auto companies and their satellite industries created Christian community. We were all basically middle-class (some a little lower and some a little upper) white middle Americans, living in the thriving middle-western section of the country. We all felt as if we were growing up in the middle of the universe and life was good.

My dad was often the negotiator with the union at his company. I frequently heard him talk about the differences he had with some of the union's demands, but I also heard him say how unions were necessary to protect workers' interests and get a fair deal from their companies. Both sides thought my father was a fair negotiator and liked him to be involved in the contract negotiations and grievance procedures. He was a popular supervisor and was known for hiring more blacks and women in his division than some other executives did. He and the workers he was responsible for seemed to all like one another.

But in his later years at Edison, I remember his being disgusted with some of the emerging executive behavior at the top of the company. And after his retirement, he became appalled by the great gaps that came to divide the compensation of corporate CEOs and their average workers. After all, these were all our friends, we all went to the same churches together, the kids all played together; we were a part of the same community. And these pay gaps were just way too big. There indeed was a social contract in Detroit, but eventually it just got broken. Tim could hardly believe the old stories of how it used to be.

DETROIT TODAY

Today, Detroit is the eleventh city in population and shrinking rapidly, from almost 2 million people to less than a million. While I was writing this book, the official unemployment rate in Detroit climbed to 28.9 percent, and everyone knew the real levels were even higher. Home prices have fallen by tens of thousands of dollars, with many people (even in my own family) underwater with their mortgages—meaning they now owe more than their homes are worth. The city of homeowners has become the city of foreclosures. When my siblings show me around their neighborhoods, they point to the many houses in foreclosure or delinquency, some where the owners have just walked away from their mortgages, and countless homes already boarded up. Commercial streets display rows and rows of shuttered storefronts. And everywhere you look, you see For Sale or For Rent signs that are now just part of the landscape of Detroit. Detroit is hardly the only city hit hard by the deep decline of the manufacturing base of the old economy; nearby Cleveland comes to mind, along with dozens of others around the country. Nor is it the only place where uncreative and short-term company thinking prevailed over decisions that might have led to more sustainability, or unions also acted in their own short-term interest in ways that enabled bad corporate choices. And Detroit is certainly not the only city or state to be dramatically driven down by a series of federal policies over the past several decades. But Detroit has become a poster child, a parable, a metaphor for these and other problems.

Nearly one-third of Detroit is now vacant land. A once densely populated city has lost over three hundred thousand[1] people since the 1980s. It is not unusual to see tents, tarps, boxes, and wooden pallets thrown together in vacant lots as shelter. In August 2009, the *Detroit Free Press* reported that three in ten people in the city were in need of a job.[2] The *Free Press* itself, due to declining revenues in January 2009, is now a much smaller version of what it used to be and does home delivery only on Thursday, Friday, and Sunday. I still can't believe that my hometown is not able to support a real daily newspaper that you can pick up at the newsstand or get on your front porch every day. The jobless rate, across the state of Michigan, in July 2009 passed 15 percent[3] as the nation climbed to an unemployment rate of almost 10 percent.

My brother, Bill Weld-Wallis, is the COO of one of the largest nonprofit organizations in the city, Neighborhood Service Organization (NSO), which provides basic services for the poor and vulnerable of Detroit. When he takes me to see some of their facilities, like a twenty-four-hour shelter and service center for homeless people nobody else will take, the scene is like something from the poorest places in the world's most impoverished countries. Hundreds of people are literally lying on the street, and hardly anybody is there to see them, still a shocking sight for most Americans. For a native of Detroit, one of the most poignant images for me was the remains of the old Tigers Stadium standing vacant and falling down as a broken reminder of what the city once was; it has recently been demolished.

Of course, there are spiritual dimensions to all the economic suffering. In May 2009, the *Detroit Free Press* published an article headlined "Faith Sustains Us in Difficult Times." Pastor Rocky Barra of the Connection Church told his congregants that the economy is "affecting more than our finance. It seems to be creating . . . an emotional disequilibrium. There is a lot of anxiety going around. There is a lot of fear." The Jewish Vocational Service in the area reported that the number of people seeking employment jumped 92 percent over the past year. But those like Eida Alawan, a sixty-nine-year-old devout Muslim who was laid off, found that it was his practice of prayer five times a day that helped him get through his several-month period of unemployment. He said, "People who have a steady diet of prayer have an even-keel type of feel that things will work out. It's just a matter of time." Scott Gendron, a regular churchgoer and GM employee concerned about losing his job said, "The less you have and the less secure you are . . . the more you have to draw upon faith. . . . It comes to a point of: What do you trust? Do you trust your finances, or do you trust God?" Before Christmas in 2008, Catholic churches in the Detroit area distributed a letter from Cardinal Adam Maida offering "some pastoral insights and suggestions about how we might prepare to celebrate Christmas this year when economic conditions are so grim."[4]

THE GREEN SHOOTS OF HOPE

But the grim statistics do not tell the entire story. And, as the "worst case scenario," Detroit could also be the unlikely place that new hopes are born. Harold Shwartz, a sixty-year-old who was laid off by an auto-parts supplier, told a reporter for *USA Today*, "Detroit isn't dying; too many people love the city to let that happen."[5] Amen. Bill Wylie-Kellermann, writing for *Sojourners* magazine, decided to ask some better questions. "What if Detroit, the vacated and rusting shell of a deindustrialized city, turns out to be the hustling forefront of urban sustainability?" What if? He goes on to say, "Another city is possible in the shell of the old. For those with eyes to see, it's actually happening."[6] And while the *Free Press* has ceased to be a real daily paper, a group of *Time* magazine reporters have

> "WHAT IF ANOTHER CITY IS POSSIBLE IN THE SHELL OF THE OLD."

bought a house together and moved in for at least a year, to report on what's happening in the city of Detroit. Maybe they too see the power of the parable, and the promise of hope rising up out of the ashes.

It's an understatement to say the world has changed since I was growing up, and I am not naive enough to think we can go back to that kind of industrial economy. But watch Detroit and some of the other places where the economic recession has hit the hardest. It may be there that the most severe economic consequences will, ironically, open the door to the more creative new solutions. And it is there where a sense of community may first be resurrected. Because, after all, in places like Detroit, all you have left is hope.

In the Depression city of Detroit, for example, a thriving new culture of urban gardening and even animal husbandry is emerging—most on squatted land and providing literal shoots of green in the cracks of the faltering auto industry. People without income are learning to grow their own food. Chickens, goats, and even cows, I'm told, are returning to the Motor City. And a barter economy is replacing the missing paychecks. It's often when people seem to have such few choices that, ironically, they begin to think outside of the box to find genuine new solutions. Sometimes, it's when our backs are most up against the wall that we start sharing our best ideas and when examples of new social leadership to create better values and solutions begin to emerge.

In a *USA Today* article about Detroit, reporter Judy Keen wrote, "There is something else, though, in this shrinking city beset by chronic poverty and the unraveling of the industry that once made it great: hope."[7] And hope is growing in some of the most unlikely places. Across the city, the vacant lots are being turned into places where lovely vegetables and even beautiful flowers are growing. Over the course of just one year, three full farms, two hundred community gardens, and four hundred family plots popped up over the city. The Capuchin friars now give away a hundred thousand plants every year to community members. Each garden not only provides locally grown food for those who need it, but opportunities for work for the unemployed and centers for the community to gather around.

The city once known for its artistic innovation and the sounds of Motown may once again grow as a city of creativity. As an evangelical teenager, I used to sneak out to dances on weekends that featured Motown artists like the Supremes, the Temptations, and Little Stevie Wonder. How can you not dance, I used to say to my concerned Evangelical parents, when you grow up in the city that has Motown!

Once again, Detroit is becoming a haven for artists seeking cheap housing, with some houses available for as little as $100 and the average cost of a house in 2009 at just $13,638.[8] "Detroit right now is just this vast, enormous canvas where anything imaginable can be accomplished,"[9] The Heidelberg Project, an artistic endeavor by Tyree Guyton, took an entire burned-out block of old homes and turned it into a giant piece of art decorated with old appliances, car parts, and shopping carts. Now this city block is raising the questions about Detroit's history and its potential future.

> "DETROIT IS JUST THIS VAST, ENORMOUS CANVAS WHERE ANYTHING IMAGINABLE CAN BE ACCOMPLISHED."

Even the shuttered factories may not be shuttered for long. Investment in green jobs could turn these factories into the epicenter of activity for a new energy economy. Assembly lines that used to produce the nation's automobiles could soon produce giant windmills for wind energy, railcars for mass-transportation systems, and new batteries instead of pistons for a new kind of car. Some imagine the Motor City producing the next generation of vehicles with new fleets of electric and hybrid cars. But that all depends on the choices we make for the new economy that is emerging.

Despite the devastation that is Detroit now, there is still a resilience, a spirit of community, and even of defiance of the devastation that is remarkably present among many long-time residents who have stayed, along with a new and almost pioneering spirit of entrepreneurial hope that has motivated some of the new residents who have just started to arrive. Whether that spirit of the long-timers is finally crushed by the weight of constant economic pressure, continual fear of crime, and hopes being always dashed; and whether enough new energy and talent arrives on time—especially with new young families—are the questions that will determine the future of my hometown. And many Detroiters, still in the city or in diaspora, find themselves doing things just to keep that hope alive, if only in symbols like the wearing of my Tigers hat as a matter of stubborn ritual—all over Washington, D.C.

REBUILDING THE WALL

The Old Testament tells the story of the prophet Nehemiah who served as a cup-bearer to the king of Persia. He and many of the Hebrew people were living in exile from the land of Israel with only a small remnant remaining by the destroyed city of Jerusalem. A report came back to Nehemiah that troubled him deeply. The report told of the devastation of the city of Jerusalem and how all the people were scattered. He went to the king and petitioned him for safe passage and the resources necessary to go back and rebuild the walls of this broken city. The king agreed to his petition, and Nehemiah returned to Jerusalem to begin the building.

Now the king had provided the resources that Nehemiah needed, the permissions necessary, and the safe passage that was crucial—all things that he could not have done without. But all of this support from the king was not enough to actually rebuild the walls of the city. It was up to Nehemiah to return and unite a scattered and discouraged people. He had to rally the people together to take responsibility for the building, to believe that it was possible to take the ruins and make something new again. The Bible gives Nehemiah's words to the people: "Then I said to them, 'You see the trouble we are in, how Jerusalem lies in ruins with its gates burned. Come, let us rebuild the wall of Jerusalem, so that we may no longer suffer disgrace.' I told them that the hand of my God had been gracious upon me, and also the words that the king had spoken to me. Then they said, 'Let us start building!' So they committed themselves to the common good." [10]

Just as Nehemiah was the prophet of the rebuilding of Jerusalem, I believe that he is the prophet for our rebuilding today. He was able to accomplish two things that were absolutely necessary for restoring the walls of a broken city, the same things that will be necessary to rebuild the foundations of our broken economy. *First*, he petitioned political power to raise the resources and provide the framework necessary for recovery. Without this support from the king, Nehemiah would not have been able to accomplish this goal. *Second*, he united the people with a vision for a city restored. The king could have provided all of the resources necessary for building, but without the people taking responsibility for accomplishing that task, it would have been for nothing.

But there were detractors. Just a few verses after the people had committed to "the common good," it says that they were mocked, ridiculed, and even accused of being traitors to the king for the work they were doing. There were vested interests in the area who benefitted from the status quo of a broken Jerusalem; to see it restored was a threat to their power. Sound familiar? Again, Nehemiah rallied the people, saying, "Do not be afraid of them. Remember the Lord, who is great and awesome, and fight for your kin, your sons, your daughters, your wives, and your homes." [11]

Nehemiah was able to rebuild with the right support from the king and when the people withstood adversity and attacks and committed themselves to the common good. Detroit too, and all of our communities, can be rebuilt with the right kind of support from our government, the private sector, and civil society; but only with people ready to overcome adversity and commit themselves to the common good. The city needs a political conversion, an economic conversion, a community conversion, and a whole lot of personal conversion as well—as we all do. The green shoots and signs are all there. It just might be the Depression city of Detroit that provides an example and vision for a country in recession to form new habits of the heart and rebuild.

TIGERTOWN

In a surprising article for *Sports Illustrated*,[12] Lee Jenkins tells the story of how the Tigers, the city's baseball team that I grew up with, became a symbol of the city's hopes and even showed a glimpse of some of the values that might lead to its recovery. At Central Methodist Church, a place where I have preached and which sits only a block from the new Comerica Park, Jenkins quotes Papa Smurf, a formerly homeless man who now volunteers at the church, exalting in how "this team—and this ballpark—is a bright light for all of us."

Jenkins quotes third-baseman Brandon Inge concerning what many expected coming into the 2009 season in the face of Detroit's economic pain: "I was here in 2003 when we lost 119 games; and a lot of nights, this stadium felt like an empty cathedral . . . I expected it to be like that again."

But like the new environment-friendly Chevy Volt, the 2009 Tigers have given a jolt to this city. In the 2009 season, the Tigers carried the hopes of a depressed city on their backs, despite their low preseason expectations. The economic forecasts haven't changed, but the whole city cheered every day for their team. Their 51–30 record at Comerica Park seemed to suggest a feeling of responsibility to their hometown fans, who really needed some good news.

In spring training, manager Jim Leyland reportedly told his players, "People are going to be spending some of their last dollars to come to these games, and we need to give them our best effort. This is not the year not to run out a ground ball." Veteran Inge concurred, "We know there are families in the stands who are fighting to keep their houses and feed their kids. . . . We take that seriously. We can't lollygag our way through a game. We have to give them a show. I really believe they are the reason that we are where we are." That spirit kept the Tigers in first place most of the season, and though the team fell just short of the playoffs, they seemed to help keep the city going though the many months of spring, summer, and fall of 2009.

I know the depressed neighborhood where Comerica is located, in the most depressed market in the Major Leagues; but my brother reported lots of excitement on game days and the feeling of hope that emanates from the ball park. The Tigers are responding to the budgets of their fans with five-dollar tickets, new five-dollar meals, and two extra five-dollar parking lots. And the team has given away more than eighty thousand tickets this year to more than two thousand nonprofit organizations. As a Little League coach, I know how much that means to a city.

Perhaps the most amazing story in the *SI* "Tigertown" article was what happened to the famous fountain beyond the center-field fence, which launches big streams of water into the sky whenever a Tiger hits a home run. Not surprisingly, GM was the fountain's proud longtime sponsor, but the publicly embarrassed automaker had to sadly tell the Tigers' management that their economic woes forced them to pull out as the historic sponsor. Quickly, two other corporations jumped on the opportunity to take the most valuable space of advertising the stadium has to offer—with one offering a million and a half dollars per year. The Tigers' owner, longtime Detroiter Mike Ilitch, considered the lucrative new deal but decided to turn it down. Instead, he put three logos on the fountain, one for GM, one for Ford, and one for Chrysler—all free of charge—over a new message, which reads "Detroit Tigers Support Our Automakers." Then each company got to send one of its employees to throw out the first pitch on opening day.

I'm not sure what to call that fountain now: perhaps a great example of restoring "The Commons," but by a baseball team in support of the companies in their city that provide jobs for their fans. It's certainly a unique phenomenon, where a pizza mogul baseball owner, whose own father worked as a tool-and-die-maker (I actually remember what that job was), chose to defy market logic and values to instead lift up the common good. Ilitch's sons say their dad regards the Tigers less as a profit-and-loss enterprise than as a "public trust." Indeed. The owner's two goals are: turning around the city and winning the World Series. Amen to both.

CONVERSION AS A PLAN FOR MORAL RECOVERY

The Detroit Tigers' centerfield home-run fountain and what it now represents stands as a good symbol of what we all need to do, each of us in our own way. It also represents a new thinking outside of the box, where we get creative, collaborate across our many public and private sectors, exercise both personal and social responsibility, and together seek to uplift the common good.

Nehemiah knew that the king's decrees were useless if the people did not fight for their values, their families, their homes, and their city. To see moral recovery, along with economic recovery, we all must make some changes. Changes deeply rooted in the values we hold must start at home, engage our communities, and transform our society. The economic crisis is not just something that has happened *to us,* but has happened *with us.* Many of us enjoyed or celebrated the fruits of it, directly or indirectly; but many others were left out altogether. But *together*, through our actions and leadership, we can all be part of the healing and change that is now needed.

> CHANGES DEEPLY ROOTED IN THE VALUES WE HOLD MUST START AT HOME, ENGAGE OUR COMMUNITIES, AND TRANSFORM OUR SOCIETY.

The changes will include new green technologies, require new kinds of jobs, and take new governmental responsibility, but that won't be enough. We will also need new habits of the heart, new directions, and new notions of ethics and mutual responsibility. These changes are nothing short of conversions to new ways of thinking and living, which will be, at the same time, personal, spiritual, civic, and political.

We have looked at some of the big conversions of the heart that might be possible as we emerge from this crisis. Change is now happening at a breathtaking pace. But it's not enough for the world to be a different place; we also need to understand how it can be a better place. If we have learned anything from this Great Recession, we have learned that greed is not enough. We need nothing less than a rediscovery of values—on Wall Street, Main Street, and Your Street. And with that, we can create a new moral compass for the new economy. It's up to us.

PART SEVEN

CHANGING
THE SCRIPT

16

A BAD
MORALITY PLAY

Just as I was finishing this book, the Dow Jones Industrial Average returned to 10,000—and Wall Street celebrated. At the same time, the nation's unemployment rate had climbed to almost 10 percent. (In my hometown of Detroit it was more like 30 percent.) The juxtaposition of those two figures—10,000 and 10 percent—was a moment of clear moral contradiction and real moral clarity. The radical disconnect between Wall Street and Main Street was abundantly clear. A bad morality play was unfolding here, and when extravagant bonuses were announced for the top executives of the banks whom the Main Street taxpayers had so recently bailed out, an outraged nation was ready to change the script.

Just a year before, the financial collapse of Wall Street investment and commercial banks triggered this Great Recession. At breathtaking speed, the federal government moved quickly to bail out the biggest and richest financial giants in the economy. We were told they were "too big to fail," and if they did, the rest of us would suffer greatly in an economic meltdown of apocalyptic proportions.

THE COUNTERFEIT BAILOUT

So we spent hundreds of billions of dollars to save the richest companies and people in America, offering them a *safety net* that we had long since decided not to grant the poorest Americans— lest they "take advantage" of it. Republicans and Democrats alike rushed to support this huge infusion of cash to Wall Street from the federal government, with few exceptions. What the banks were supposed to do with our money was to start lending again—which they had stopped doing—to creditworthy businesses and homeowners for whom critical capital had dried up.

The American people were asked to trust the smart people who knew best and to count on the banks to restore the credit flow to individuals and small businesses that needed it. But some banks bought up (with our money) stocks, bonds, and other assets at rock-bottom prices and then made a killing in profits as the stock market stabilized and began to rise again. Then, to congratulate themselves for recognizing the opportunity for making a profit, they gave out record compensation bonuses to themselves while wages for the rest of the country continued to fall and more and more people found themselves without a job at all. It was a morality play almost too unbelievably bad to be true; yet that is exactly what happened.

Banks were bailed out with billions of taxpayer funds for loans that we were told were absolutely essential to avoid a complete system failure—with few strings attached. While no one seemed to like the idea of bailing out those who had made the shortsighted decisions that precipitated our economic crash, we went along because, in a crisis, everyone needs to sacrifice.

There is continued disagreement as to how the bailouts were

designed (quite poorly), but a lot of smart people, whom I respect, still believe that doing something was necessary to save
our country and the world financial system from a much greater
crash. All of it, however, would have been much easier to take if
those who had advocated most fer-
vently for bailouts to return our financial system to the status quo were not
the ones who had made millions from
the status quo of the financial system
in the first place. To then learn that
instead of supporting homeowners
and small businesses, the money went
to corporate profiteering, resulting in
record bonuses to the top financial
managers, was just too much to bear.
To see that Wall Street is now having a
party while the rest of the country
continues to buckle down, sacrifice,

> ALL OF IT
> WOULD HAVE
> BEEN EASIER TO
> TAKE IF THOSE
> WHO HAD
> ADVOCATED
> FOR BAILOUTS
> WERE NOT THE
> ONES WHO HAD
> MADE MILLIONS
> FROM THE
> STATUS QUO.

and do what is necessary to make it through all this is just too
much. It is very clear that this is immoral, and now the country
needs to ask, should it also be illegal?

Of course, I am aware of the conventional economic analysis
that the stock market often comes back faster than jobs do, but
those conventional rationales are not adequate to explain the
current phenomena we are seeing on Wall Street these days, nor
do they acknowledge the moral failings here. The predominance
of the paper economy over the productive economy was a root
cause of this recession, and that preference is one of the core realities that must be changed. Real people with real jobs who do
real work have to be the foundation of a healthy economy, rather
than the speculative gamblers who just move our money around.

ACCUSATIONS OF MARXISM

Yet today, if anyone questions whether these bonuses are actually deserved and whether we, as the taxpayers who financed all of this, should be able to share in any of the profits, they are accused of being a socialist, a communist, or worse. CNBC *Mad Money*'s Jim Cramer, whose economic morality was discussed earlier in the book and who always has a way with words, was asked what he thought about the divergence between Wall Street and Main Street with the DOW at 10,000 and Main Street in shambles. His answer:

> I went for a master's degree in communism, and we learned about these things . . . Lenin, when he came in 1917, felt that the bankers were making too much money, and he confiscated all their wealth. The peasantry felt terrific about it. The peasantry reacted positively. . . . It traced out well and the peasantry was rejoicing and the bankers—many of them were killed—and there was a terrific, terrific surge of opinion that Lenin was a great man.[1]

What? Cramer was suggesting that to question such Wall Street profiteering was to opt for the economic solutions of Lenin's Soviet state. What a morality play this was becoming!

Questioning billions in bonuses funded by taxpayer dollars while unemployment continues to climb is a matter of commonsense balance, not a slippery slope to killing millions as Stalin did. This is the false choice we have been sold for many years, but one that I believe many people can now see through: either accept this outrageous corporate behavior as a necessary component of capitalism, without complaint or action, or suffer the evil and oppression wrought upon the world by men like Lenin, Stalin, and Mao.

REASONS TO BE ANGRY

The anger that many Americans feel comes from a few different places, none of them Marxist. The first is that the behavior of the rich on Wall Street is an affront to our basic understanding of values like commitment, integrity, fairness, and loyalty to others besides themselves. We at least hoped there would be enough people in the financial industry who would take the opportunity given to them by the bailout to help rescue our country and the world from the brink of financial disaster, and not pay themselves more millions in bonuses to do it.

> THE BEHAVIOR OF THE RICH ON WALL STREET IS AN AFFRONT TO OUR BASIC UNDER-STANDING OF VALUES.

Every day we are surrounded by teachers, nurses, ordinary workers, small-business owners, firefighters, police officers, and other public servants (and, most poignantly, servicemen and servicewomen in war zones) who are smart and talented, work hard, and make many sacrifices because they want to be productive and contributive members of their society and country—working for more than just getting a paycheck. Of course they want to be compensated; of course they want to be rewarded for good work. But when times get tough, they don't just walk away or demand millions in bonuses; they buckle down because it is the right thing to do. Teach For America isn't harder to get into than many Ivy League colleges because it pays out millions in bonuses, but because there are so many young people who believe that motivation to do good work does not come solely from a salary.

And as someone who has worked with the poorest of the poor in our country for most of my life, I get angry for another reason. For years I heard from legislators or television pundits that they would not support food stamps for the hungry, welfare for the poor, or housing for the homeless because, if they did, the poor people would just take advantage of it all. Even though fraud in food stamps or other government programs costs the American taxpayer only pennies a year, those arguments worked almost every time. Now, instead of a safety net for the poor and middle class in our country, we have one for some of the wealthiest people in the world, and one that costs us many times more—not pennies, but billions of dollars.

Let's name some of the worse culprits. Goldman Sachs, who borrowed $10 billion from the U.S. government and later repaid it (with some of the windfall profits made from investing with our taxpayer dollars), is on track, as I write, to pay out $23 billion in 2009 in bonuses, twice what it paid in 2008.[2] Consumer banks, while not involved in the same tricks as investment banks like Goldman Sachs, have acted irresponsibly as well. Bank of America and Citigroup, who together accepted $90 billion in bailout funds in 2008 (which they have yet to return) paid out $8.66 billion in bonuses.[3] (Meanwhile, the average bank teller at Bank of America makes just $10.73 an hour, or just over $22,000 a year.)

SOME OF THOSE BANKS THAT WERE TOO BIG TO FAIL HAVE NOW BECOME TOO IMMORAL TO SUCCEED.

The time has come to say that some of those banks that were too big to fail have now become too immoral to succeed. We must move from not allowing them to fail, to not allowing their failed behaviors to continue. I believe it is time to consider taking our money out of the big banks and credit unions to protect both our money and our integrity. Our ability to choose different banks, when we see those failures, is an important part of our market system working, and perhaps it will also be one way to help change the behavior of the market as well.

DEMOCRACY IN ACTION

But our personal actions are not enough—we need government to help rebalance the three-legged stool. What has become clear in this bad morality play is that the *ethos* of Wall Street will not change from the inside. The arrogance and utter shamelessness of the Wall Street financial giants have now been revealed—and in such a short time after their economic and moral collapse. It's clear that Wall Street ha learned nothing, wants to learn nothing, and instead just wants to go back to the same old behaviors.

Keeping true to his promise to reevaluate his previously held economic thinking with the changing reality of today, Alan Greenspan in October 2009 said, "If they're too big to fail, they're too big . . . In 1911 we broke up Standard Oil—so what happened? The individual parts became more valuable than the whole. Maybe that's what we need to do."[4] The government breakup of behemoth banks flies in the face of free-market fundamentalism, but now even Greenspan has become a proponent of this measure to find our balance again. Others have wondered if the government should step in and increase the liability of bank executives for the decisions that they make. It would allow them to be rewarded when their work pays off but make sure they have skin in the game when their decisions turn out to be reckless. A balanced stool might also need new regulations around the revolving door between government regulators and lobbying for the industry they are supposed to regulate.

The morality play continued. In the first six months of 2009 the financial services industry spent $223 million lobbying Congress to *fight* any additional regulation, restrictions, or requirements and was on track to more than double that spending for the rest of the year.[5] While this kind of money being spent to fight fundamental public accountability is formidable, it has yet to render our democratic processes beyond repair. And now more than ever, we must all see to it that our democratic institutions are more responsive to the needs of real people than to the special interest industry lobbies.

This will indeed be a fundamental test of democracy in our time. Will we be a government "of the people, by the people, and for the people"? Or will we be a nation "of the money, by the money, and for the money"? The choices are becoming more and more clear. What is most clear in this bad morality play is that the characters, roles, and story lines remain constant, no matter what happens. But many in the audience have seen enough and believe it is time to change the script.

EPILOGUE

NOTES FROM THE NEXT GENERATION

TIM KING

My grandmother tells a story about a man who came to her back, kitchen door, looking for food. She was a young girl at the time, cooking dinner with her mother. The country was still in the midst of the Great Depression, and hungry people were no surprise. What surprised her, and surprised me, was her mother's response to this man's request. My grandmother's mother, my great-grandmother, graciously invited the man into the kitchen and offered him a seat at the table. She and my grandmother went to the pantry to gather more food, a plate, and utensils for his meal.

They returned a few minutes later with a plate of food to find that the man had left and taken most of their evening's dinner from the stove with him. My great-grandmother, without a word, silently began preparing dinner with the food that was left. My grandmother protested that the man had stolen their food! But my great-grandmother, a woman I never knew, but whose wisdom I now know well, explained a simple lesson to my grandmother: he was in need, we have enough, and we should share it.

Dinner for my grandmother was sparse that night, but the lesson stayed with her and our entire family ever since. Part of being a Christian, part of being a good neighbor, means that you give to those in need, even if that means dinner is a little smaller some nights. The experiences my grandmother had during the Great Depression shaped her values for a lifetime. The hardships in the world around her as she grew up became lessons she shared with her children, her grandchildren, and now her great-grandchildren.

Growing up, I could never fully understand why my grand-parents could recall the exact time and place they were when they heard about Pearl Harbor, or the stories they would tell time and again about the Great Depression. Now I understand. Some moments and events are so significant, so important, that they become emblazoned into our own minds and onto a national psyche, and for better or worse form a generation's spirit and character. Sometimes, these events happen in a moment as with Pearl Harbor or 9/11. Others are prolonged over the course of years like the Great Depression and now, the Great Recession. They are significant enough and impactful enough that their influence is felt for decades to come.

My generation will forever be shaped by the falling of the twin towers and is right now being shaped by the Great Recession. The choices we make both personally and collectively in response to those great challenges will largely determine our character for years to come.

There are, I believe, two primary spiritual responses that all of us, but my generation in particular, must choose between in the Great Recession. The first is to build walls, the second to grow roots. The first, to react out of fear; the second, to act out of hope. The first is to regress into a position of weakness; the second, to choose a position of strength.

Fear is a natural instinct and normal reaction to dangerous or quickly changing situations. But when fear is turned from a natural warning system into a normative way of being, living, and acting, it destroys instead of keeping us safe. Fear is what drives us to build higher and higher walls between us and our neighbors in the hopes that separation from others means security for ourselves. It is a sign of weakness when we continue to react out of fear. It shows that whatever the situation is, it is the situation that controls our actions and dictates what we do.

The maxims of "Greed is good," "It's all about me," and "I want it now" are all walls that could be built higher in the coming years. In reaction to economic instability, some people will turn to greed in the belief that if they just keep accumulating more, it will someday make them feel safe and secure. They will turn inward, focus on themselves, scared to share and scared to be vulnerable for fear of what may be taken from them. Immediate gratification will overcome thoughts of a better world for generations to come.

Growing roots is a radical act. The word *radical* comes from the Latin word *radis*, which means roots. Roots represent the center, the heart, the basis from which plants, ideas, religions, and even countries draw life. When in response to a challenge we choose to grow roots, it means we choose to move past what is on the surface and dig beneath to the source. It is a place of strength because we set the terms and determine for ourselves how we should act in the future instead of letting the challenge determine our reaction. Growing roots is based in hope, because it shows a strength and a belief that these challenges will be overcome.

We have the opportunity to grow and strengthen roots by

learning that "Enough is enough," "We're in it together," and by having a "seventh-generation mind-set." As this book illustrates, these are not new values that we need to create for ourselves. The challenge is admitting that our parents and grandparents might actually know more than we think.

For years I watched my dad calculate miles per gallon for his car on gas station receipts, and without a word I learned the importance of conserving our resources. My mom had all her kids out in our backyard garden, building raised beds for the vegetables, and even learning how to can and freeze the produce—skills that might be helpful if I ever end up with an urban garden. Recently, my grandmother's long-lost nephew who had been adopted at birth tracked us, his biological family, down. He is an ardent atheist and believes that organized religion is one of the great scourges of the world today. After a week with his aunt, he said he would change his mind about religion if we could only show him a few more Christians who loved people like my Grammy Ruth.

As a young man, St. Augustine prayed, "Lord, make me pure—but not yet." I couldn't agree with him more, and I do hope the good Lord lets me take my time in getting there. While looking at some of the lessons in this book, I have prayed, "Lord, let me learn them—but not yet." After all, I just started earning a salary only a few short years ago, so I haven't had all of the opportunities to be greedy that many of my elders have enjoyed. But to relegate this conversation on values to only the generations that have had their fun and made their mistakes is to miss an opportunity. Living out these values and being virtuous is something that is formed over a lifetime. These values do not appear out of nowhere when we are ready, but are part of good habits we develop day after day.

The good news is that I already hear these conversations all the time. My older sister works in cancer research and is going back to school for a counseling degree. My brother is a high-school teacher at a low-income school on the South Side of Chicago. My little sister called me on the first day of college, thrilled that she could sign up to work with homeless people on the streets. I have friends who are in law school for the express purpose of ending human trafficking; others have started nonprofits in the United States to support development projects in third-world countries. I get to travel with Jim across the country and hear the questions from high school and college students, as well as young professionals, asking about how they can take their gifts and talents and meet the needs of the world around them. Asking how they can be better businesspeople, innovators in nonprofits, or leaders in the faith community.

I see a lot of reasons to believe that my generation will choose to grow roots and not to build walls. But we will also have to face the challenge of making sure these changes and conversations are not just a phase of life, but a way of living life. The challenge of meeting the needs of the world can't be put on a short checklist of things to do after college along with backpacking through Europe. Life will certainly change, jobs will change, and other demands and responsibilities will arise—how my generation lives these things out in twenty years will look different than it does today. But that does not mean that these values, hopes, and goals are a passing fad. Roots should provide growth for a lifetime. My hope is that just as some of my grandmother's best values were passed on to me, I will have the chance to pass along my best values to a new generation.

STUDY GUIDE AND
MORAL EXERCISES

I t is increasingly clear that people are *angry* about this economic crisis and its consequences. Many more simply feel
helpless. I think the two are deeply related. Things have
happened that we don't like, decisions have been implemented
that we had no voice in, and choices that affect the direction of
our country are made—usually without any real public debate
or knowledge of pertinent discussions. The most significant decisions seem to be made by only a few people, but with consequences for a lot of people. And it's not only about what
happened on Wall Street—how taxpayers were straddled with
bailing out those who made bad choices and what the financial
giants have done with our money. It's also about the things we
are bombarded with in everyday culture, like the ads that make
my twelve-year-old son cringe when he is just trying to watch
the Major League Baseball playoffs. It's about the *moral* choices
made in public budgets regarding what is important and what
is not. It's about the *rules of the game* that are often quietly
changed. It's about the big decisions regarding economic fairness, war, and peace. And it's about the huge cultural shifts that
most of us never voted on, had any say in, or were even told
about.

People get even angrier and feel more helpless when they see
that many decisions—which have big consequences for them
and their kids—are in fact made by politicians whose campaigns

are financed by the same people who brought down the economy. Yet somehow they have managed to come out on top again while so many Americans are still in very desperate straits. The game does feel rigged—and it is. People feel let down by the democracy they used to trust. Though our country still has the *forms* of democracy, it has lost much of its *substance*. So we feel helpless, angry, or both.

Change *begins* when people make different choices *individually*. Change *grows* when people make different choices *together*. And when the critical mass of those who are making different choices gets big enough, change becomes a *social movement*. It is those movements that change history more than anything else. But you must first believe in the *power of choice* in order to start making different choices.

Anyone who has ever suffered with addiction knows the power and promise of making different choices and being supported in those choices. And in reality, the crisis we now face in our economy and society stems from behaviors that are indeed addictive, yet have been systematically encouraged. To change those systems and the habits that support them, we have to start making different choices. The first change we need to make is to channel our anger into energy and convert our helplessness into hope.

Change never starts until some of us *believe* that change is possible and then bet our lives on it. But usually, believing comes from *doing*—from making different choices personally, in our families, in our congregations, in our communities, and in our nation. And these choices are not just small things to make us feel better about our personal lives; they are together the very things that add up to the big social changes. For example, the milestone political victories of the Civil Rights Act of 1964 or the Voting Rights Act of 1965 were not simply the result of votes in Congress or even the marches in Birmingham and Selma, but were finally caused by personal choices and decisions made by literally millions of people—some small and some at great sacrifice and cost. The same is true for every other social movement that has significantly changed a status quo that had caused people to feel angry or helpless. Choices do result in change.

This book has tried not only to describe what is wrong, but to explore how to make things right. Change is preceded by commitments, new practices, and new disciplines—on all our parts. So we conclude this book with some study questions to bring the focus back to the values you want to rediscover, as well as some moral exercises you can do to begin the process of making choices that make changes. Just as physical exercise produces results only when it becomes a habit, so *must moral* exercise become a discipline if we are to achieve lasting change.

INTRODUCTION

STUDY QUESTIONS

1. Has your life changed since the market crash? How about the lives of those around you? What do these changes look like?
2. Jim says that the most important question isn't "When will the crisis end?" but "How will this crisis change us?" What is the difference between those two questions? Why is this difference important?
3. What conversations have you had about values that were inspired by the economic changes? What evidence (if any) have you seen that makes you think those in government have reassessed their values? What about Wall Street?
4. Jim tells the story of a church in Ohio that responded to families out of work in their congregation by raising

$625,000 to help get people in the church and community back to work. What similar stories of community-serving churches have you heard?

MORAL EXERCISE: CHOOSE HOPE

Every choice we make is motivated by something. Sometimes these motivations are good, sometimes they are bad, and other times they are somewhere in between. Large groups of people can be moved to action by a common positive vision for the future or by just finding a group or a person to blame for their problems.

List some recent decisions you have made. What motivated them? What about decisions being made at your place of work or worship? What informed those decisions? Are there ways the decisions could have been made differently?

1. SUNDAY SCHOOL WITH JON STEWART

STUDY QUESTIONS

1. Jim says, "Crisis is a good time to clarify the meaning of many things." Do you agree? In what ways has our current economic crisis helped you find clarity? Confusion? (page 13)
2. The story of "The Money Changers" was used by FDR in his first inaugural address. What parallels do you see between that story and today's situation? (page 15)
3. What is the difference between a personal sin and social sin? (page 21)
4. What does Jim mean by his statement that "the common good is our own good"? How is this true? (page 21)

MORAL EXERCISE: KNOW YOUR SCRIPTURES

In order to bring about both an economic and moral recovery, we need to rediscover our oldest and best values. These values are not new principles, but many have been forgotten. This book draws from the deep wells of Christian, Jewish, and Muslim traditions, but there is much more that our Scriptures can teach us about the issues raised in the pages of this book.

What other lessons can you learn from your faith tradition or even from other traditions? Take the time to explore the Bible, Hebrew Scriptures, and the Koran to discover how those ancient values apply today. Start or join a regular study with some friends. Other resources are available on the www.sojo.net website to help you get started.

2. WHEN THE MARKET BECAME GOD

STUDY QUESTIONS

1. What is an idol? Have you seen "the market" become an idol in your own life? What other idols do we often turn to? (page 27)
2. Harvey Cox said that "the market" has become like the "Hound of Heaven" and pursues us everywhere we go. What does he mean by that? Have you ever felt "pursued" by marketing, consumerism, and more stuff to buy? (page 29)
3. Adam Smith, the father of modern economics, wrote about moral philosophy before he ever wrote about economics. How have our moral values been replaced by market values? (page 34)
4. In what areas have you seen "the market" encroach on

your life or society in bad or unhealthy ways? What checks and balances have you put in your life to monitor the reach of "the market"? (page 35)

MORAL EXERCISE: BECOME AN ICONOCLAST

There probably aren't any churches out there that have literally replaced the Cross with a golden calf, but others "idols" are evidenced in the lives of individuals through how they live and set their priorities. Idols can creep into our lives without us knowing. Sometimes we need the insight and accountability of others to help identify where this has happened in our own lives.

Find a friend or family member you can trust, and talk through areas of your life where you rely upon idols rather than God. In what ways have you been tempted to replace your moral values with market values? What might this look like at work? At school? At home? At your church?

3. GREED IS GOOD

STUDY QUESTIONS

1. Who are your cultural role models? How about your children's? Do you ever find yourself or your family modeling the bad behavior of the wealthy on TV? (page 42)
2. There aren't too many people who will agree aloud with Gordon Gekko that "greed is good." But in what ways do we agree by how we live our lives and set our priorities? (page 43)
3. Jim talks about the pressure he and his wife, Joy, felt to take on more debt. Have you felt similar pressure?

Where does that pressure come from and why is it so hard to fight? (page 45)

4. What is "conspicuous consumption"? In what ways might you have based all or part of your identity on "treasures here on earth"? (page 47)

MORAL EXERCISE: CHOOSE WHERE TO INVEST YOUR MONEY

Joy and I made the decision that none of the big national banks that got huge bailouts and then gave shameless bonuses to their executives were the right place for our money. We wanted to bring our business to institutions that we could trust, that better reflected our values, and that were more connected to our local community.

Who are you banking with? Where is your money invested? How about your retirement account? College savings account? Go through your finances and determine whether the places you have your money reflect your values. If not, use some of the resources on the website www.sojo.net to find places that better reflect your values.

4. IT'S ALL ABOUT ME

STUDY QUESTIONS

1. Jim says that our country's tradition of "individual liberty and responsibility has been replaced by a culture of narcissism." What does he mean by that? (page 51)
2. Alan Greenspan, former chairman of the Federal Reserve, told a congressional committee that for forty years he had operated under the assumption that "self-interest" would regulate lending institutions. He then admit-

ted that he was wrong to think this. Why has Greenspan changed his mind? Why is that important? (page 52)

3. What is *hubris*? In what ways have you seen hubris factor into the economic collapse? Have you ever experienced it yourself? (page 53)

4. Jim talks about his children and the problems that result when "I am special" turns into "I am an exception." When "I believe in myself" becomes "I do not believe in others." Why do these mind-sets cause problems? What are the important differences between the two versions of each viewpoint? (page 54)

5. Why do we often fail to be the Good Samaritan? (page 59)

MORAL EXERCISE: REACH OUT TO YOUR NEIGHBORS

When we begin with the ethic that we are all in this together, it changes the way we treat those who are immediately around us. One of the greatest strengths of our society is when we as neighbors look out for each other. But increasingly, people do not even know those who live right beside them.

Go ahead. Try it. Introduce yourself to the neighbors you don't know. Maybe some fresh-baked cookies or an invitation to dinner will break the ice.

5. I WANT IT NOW

STUDY QUESTIONS

1. We are often able to get what we want when we want it, but as the comedian Louis C.K. pointed out, what we want doesn't always make us happy. Jim was challenged

by a friend who asked if all the convenience of technology has given us more time to pray. What do you think? Have technological advances allowed you to do more of what's really important? (page 66)

2. What is the role of debt in your life? Is it a service, or has it become master? (page 68)

3. Efficiency is an important value of the market, but it is not necessarily a family value. When can the desire to get things done quickly become harmful or even dangerous? (page 70)

4. How does our "I want it now" ethic affect the planet? (page 72)

MORAL EXERCISE: BALANCE SCREEN TIME WITH FAMILY TIME

Screens are everywhere in our life today—making us both more efficient and more distracted. In our families there is often a constant tension between the time our kids spend in front of screens and the time they spend reading, playing outside, using their imagination, or enjoying quality time with their family.

Think about how the TV, computer, and phone screens in your life become distractions. Create a schedule with rules and guidelines so that you and your family can experience some screen-free time, and replace that time with specific activities for quality time with family and friends.

6. WHEN THE GAPS GET TOO BIG

STUDY QUESTIONS

1. What are some of the reasons our society has become increasingly unequal?

2. What negative results does extreme inequality have for society as a whole?

3. Jim says that "The Great Lie" claims that "those who are wealthy are so because they are responsible and righteous, and those who are poor must be irresponsible, or even immoral." Why is this a lie, and what is the truth about the moral distinctions of the wealthy and the poor? (page 88)

MORAL EXERCISE: GIVE GLOBALLY

Aid and development are becoming smarter and more sustainable. *Compassionate* and *smart* will be the new watchwords of global development. *Effective, transparent,* and *accountable* are the new operational values. While it is easiest to see the problems closest to us, we need to remember that our global neighbors also matter. This economic downturn has meant struggle and great hardship for many in the United States; but for those in other areas of the world, it has become a struggle of life and death.

While things might be tough for you and your family right now, consider giving sacrificially to those in the world who have been hit the hardest. Check the website for the most effective organizations for channeling your giving.

7. ON LISTENING TO CANARIES

STUDY QUESTIONS

1. Why does Jim refer to the poor in our society as the "canary in the coal mine"? What are some signs that the canary isn't doing well?

2. *Redistribution* is a word that rubs a lot of people the wrong way. What were your thoughts when you read that not only leaders from the Old Testament (page 93), the New Testament (page 94), and the early Church talked about redistributing wealth, but also America's founding fathers? (page 95)

3. Jim talks about a "Bible full of holes." In what ways does your Bible have holes in it? How can you put it back together? (page 100)

MORAL EXERCISE: LISTEN TO THE CANARIES

This book illustrates that the poorest and most vulnerable in our country provide early warning signals that something is not right. Changes in our economy, our culture, and our government's policy are necessary to address these issues. There are many long-standing organizations whose mission is to listen to the canaries and make it possible for individuals and congregations to get involved (chapters 7 and 14).

Using the resources listed on the www.sojo.net website, find an organization you can trust that connects with your passions and commitments to overcome poverty. That organization's staff, programs, and websites will help you learn about their public policy and keep you informed about relevant news. They can also let you know when to contact your political representatives and which current policies affect the organization. Making a long-term commitment to an organization, by participating in its events and conferences, and keeping in touch with its staff, can be a great benefit to you and the organization. Be sure to have conversations about these issues with your children to instill in them an ethic for overcoming poverty.

8. ENOUGH IS ENOUGH

STUDY QUESTIONS

1. How can the ethic of "enough is enough" replace "greed is good"?
2. What are the things that truly satisfy you? Make you happy? Make you feel secure? What does Jesus have to say about these things? (page 109)
3. In a crisis, it can be easy to think only of ourselves. What does the story of the five loaves and two fish have to say in response? (page 117)
4. According to one study, the poor are the most generous segment of our society. Does this challenge your own assumptions? Your attitude toward giving? How do you think their generosity is possible? (page 118)

MORAL EXERCISE: AUDIT YOUR LIFESTYLE

Instead of paying for things we don't need with money we don't have, we need to remember that simplicity is actually a gift. Simplicity is not about restricting the abundance of life, but about cutting out the things that aren't really important so that life can be lived more fully. Living more simply can be both a regular practice and a spiritual discipline (chapters 3 and 8).

Find something in your life that is more a want than a need, and try giving it up for a while. Perhaps it is your many trips to the coffee shop or going out to eat too much. Or maybe it's expensive entertainment, an extra car, or overly expensive vacations. Next time you are shopping, before you pull each item off the shelf, ask yourself if the item is a want or a need? Spend the extra time or money you save on other priorities, or give it away to an organiza-

tion or cause you believe in. Involve people you trust in helping you with your lifestyle audit.

9. WE'RE IN IT TOGETHER

STUDY QUESTIONS

1. How does *It's a Wonderful Life* tell a different story of what our communities and country could be when compared to many of the stories we hear about in the news today? (page 121)
2. What can we learn from the old story of *Soup from a Stone*? (page 123) What about the common practice of potlucks? (page 123)
3. Shariah banking and the Nehemiah Homes project show that our religious principles can also make good business sense. What other ways can our values not only be good for our souls but good for business and the economy? (page 126)

MORAL EXERCISE: WELCOME STRANGERS AND INTERACT WITH NEIGHBORS

Those of us who have been given much, are expected to give much. Hospitality—welcoming neighbors and strangers into our homes and lives—is one of the ways we are able to share the good gifts we have been given. You can make your home a place of hospitality for your immediate neighbors and others who might be in need (chapters 8 and 9)

In order to get to know your neighbors you might host a dinner, a neighborhood gathering, or even a group to read this book together. A bigger challenge would be to open up your home to a family—maybe a homeless mother and her children in need of a safe and supportive place to get their lives back together. I've even heard of young people opening up their apartments to national and international "couch surfers" traveling through who need a place to stay.

10. THE SEVENTH-GENERATION MIND-SET

STUDY QUESTIONS

1. What is a "moral hazard"? Describe a situation when you found yourself affected by moral hazards. (page 134)
2. Why is it so hard to remember the Sabbath? (page 136)
3. God commanded the Hebrew people to leave their fields unplanted once every seven years. You might not have a farm, but how can you apply this principle of caring for creation in your own life? (page 138)
4. Jim talks about his son's heroes and how they influence him. Who are your heroes? Your children's? (page 143)

MORAL EXERCISE: MAKE A SEVENTH-GENERATION COMMITMENT

It's easy to get caught up in the demands of today. What is happening now can quickly dominate our thinking and our actions. But what about how our actions affect our children or even our grandchildren? How will what we do today change our planet, for better or worse, for generations to come?

Make a seventh-generation commitment. Determine where in your life you can make a sacrifice today that will benefit others for years to come. Perhaps this means letting go of what seems important today so you can spend time with your family and affect them for a life time. Or maybe it means slowing down and investing in young leaders around you.

11. THE CLEAN-ENERGY ECONOMY CONVERSION

STUDY QUESTIONS

1. What positive changes involving "creation care" have you seen in the lives of others? In your own life?
2. What could a clean-energy conversion look like? (page 147)
3. Jim describes his experience with his family on Block Island. What kinds of experiences do you have in appreciating God's creation? (page 150)

MORAL EXERCISE: GO GREEN—EVEN WHEN IT'S NOT EASY

We have all heard about the importance of changing our incandescent lightbulbs to more energy efficient compact fluorescent lightbulbs, but changes that will impact generations to come need to go deeper. We need to challenge ourselves to make bigger and even more sacrificial changes to ensure that our environment is preserved for years to come.

Is it time for you to consider more environment-friendly methods of transportation? You might buy a hybrid car, share a car, or ride a bike. Maybe you can walk more and drive less, or forgo travel when possible. You might think about limiting your household to one car (which means collaborating with other families and friends), or even getting rid of your car altogether and switching to public trans-

portation. You could look into options for energy-efficient appliances, weatherizing your home, or installing solar panels.

12. FAMILY MATTERS CULTURE

STUDY QUESTIONS

1. Jim says there has been "a war declared on our families." What does he mean by that? Do you agree? (page 157)
2. TVs, cell phones, and video games keep getting cheaper and more portable, while family time keeps becoming harder to come by. Why is that? How can you counter that trend? (page 162)
3. What dangers does the PA Child Care scandal warn us of? (page 163)

MORAL EXERCISE: CALENDARS AND BUDGETS ARE MORAL DOCUMENTS

A budget is actually a moral document that reveals what and who are most important to a family, a church, a city, a state, or a nation. Being a father, I have learned that a calendar is also a moral document. Our calendars show how we spend our time, and our budgets show how we spend our money.

Make a list of the priorities in your life. Then go through your calendar and budget with your spouse, a family member, trusted friends, or even your church small group, and list the top ways you are spending your time and your money. How do your budget and calendar match up with your life priorities, and how are they different? You may be in for some surprises. What changes could you make in how you spend your time and money to ensure your expenditures match your priorities?

13. THE MEANING OF WORK AND THE ETHIC OF SERVICE

STUDY QUESTIONS

1. How do you view work? Your job? How does Jim define work? (page 172)
2. Fifty-eight percent of the Harvard class of 2007 opted for careers in finance or consulting, with a full 20 percent going into investment banking. What does this say about the goals of this new generation? Do you think these statistics define the next generation, or is it better represented by the thousands who sign up for programs like Teach for America? (page 176)
3. What is civil society? How do we build it? Why is it radical? (page 178)

MORAL EXERCISE: CHOOSE MEANINGFUL WORK AND OPPORTUNITIES FOR SERVICE

Work can be more than what we do to get a paycheck. Most jobs have opportunities for deeper meaning or commitment to the community or the world around you—from corporations that encourage philanthropy and service to those that embed social statements and commitments into their DNA. Service opportunities outside the workplace also abound. Every year around Thanksgiving and Christmas, volunteers and donations flood into food pantries and homeless shelters to try and make sure every person in our country has something to celebrate. But service is about more than a once-a-year gesture or a holiday activity.

It might be time for you to consider the big decision to change jobs or change your job. Are there employment opportunities that better reflect your gifts, interests, passions, and priorities? Are there ways you can help your own place of work change its thinking or practices to reflect better values?

You can also look into local volunteer opportunities that you can share with your family and friends. This is a great way to involve your children in something that will change them. Volunteering allows you to build relationships with the people you serve and encourage others to get involved as well. Resources on the www.sojo.net website can help you get started—but there might even be a service opportunity at your church or place of work.

14. REGAINING OUR BALANCE

STUDY QUESTIONS

1. What does it mean for society to have lost its "balance"? What are the signs that we have lost our balance? (page 183)
2. How does sin affect the economy? What are some ways to check its influence? (page 188)
3. How can the government help create a fair playing field?
4. How can the church work as a check to the market and ensure that the government doesn't encroach too far on our freedoms? (page 194)

MORAL EXERCISE: USE YOUR CONSUMER POWER

The choices we make about the things we buy really do shape the demands of the market. If as consumers we demand certain products—like fair-trade coffee or chocolate or locally grown produce—we can create incentives for businesses to make sure their products live up to those standards.

In your everyday purchases, try to find alternatives that reflect your values and priorities. For larger or regular purchases, take the time to research where things are coming from and the practices of the companies you are buying from. Join with campaigns that are trying to harness and channel consumer power to change corporate behavior on moral issues. The www.sojo.net website has more information on how your purchases can better represent your values.

15. THE PARABLE OF DETROIT AND THE GREEN SHOOTS OF HOPE

STUDY QUESTIONS

1. What are some of the signs of hope Jim sees in Detroit? What signs do you see in your own community? (page 205)
2. What parallels do you see between the story of Nehemiah and the situation our country is in today? (page 207)
3. What lessons of unity can we learn from the story of "Tigertown"? Are there ways to replicate that kind of cooperation in our own communities? (page 211)

MORAL EXERCISE: TEND TO THE GREEN SHOOTS

Headlines often focus on what is going wrong, but as we can see from Detroit, there are already green shoots of hope across the country. Communities are pulling together, neighbors are supporting one another, and entrepreneurs are discovering new modes of innovation.

Take some time to go through your local paper with an eye toward finding the shoots of hope. Find out if faith communities or nonprofits in your neighborhood are taking creative approaches to helping those in need. If you hear about an interesting program or initiative, maybe it's time to help the green shoots grow by replicating it yourself! Be a messenger of hope, and commit your time and energy to help create a moral compass for a new economy.

16. A BAD MORALITY PLAY

STUDY QUESTIONS

1. As the "Bad Morality Play" continues to unfold, how has the plot changed? Who are the new characters? New challenges?
2. When you hear about the economy in the news, do you feel like there is anything you can do to make a difference? What would make a difference? (page 223)
3. Jim says that these times could be a test of our democratic processes. He asks, "Will we be a government of the people, by the people, and for the people? Or will we be a nation of the money, by the money, and for the money?" What is the difference in these two approaches, and what can you do to shape the process?

MORAL EXERCISE: JOIN A CAMPAIGN

Person after person, community after community, making choices for change and joining together in a campaign can be a powerful force. A well-organized campaign that targets change in specific areas can have a more powerful impact than you might think.

Consider joining a local campaign, such as bringing a farmers' market to your area or working to improve the schools in your town. Join a national campaign that focuses on issues addressed in this book, like concern over the influence of big money in politics, out-of-control bonuses, or consumer-protection issues. International campaigns include promoting Fair Trade products from developing nations, ending extreme poverty, or fighting global sexual and economic slavery. Again, check the www.sojo.net website for some of the best campaigns.

NOTES

INTRODUCTION

1. http://www.cleveland.com/nation/index.ssf/2009/04/suburban_columbus_church_colle.html; http://www.vineyardcolumbus.org/resources/sermons/sermon_resources.asp?year=2009, April 5, 2009.

CHAPTER 1: SUNDAY SCHOOL WITH JON STEWART

1. To watch the complete show: http://blog.sojo.net/2009/03/13/sunday-school-with-jon-stewart.
2. http://www.bartleby.com/124/pres49.html.
3. John 2:13–22.
4. Benedict XVI, "Caritas in Veritate," July 7, 2009.

CHAPTER 2: WHEN THE MARKET BECAME GOD

1. Exodus 32:4b NLT.
2. "Wiesel Lost 'Everything' to Madoff," Portfolio.com, February 6, 2009, http://www.portfolio.com/executives/2009/02/26/Elie_Wiesel_and_Bernard_Madoff/.
3. Harvey Cox, "The Market as God," http://www.theatlantic.com/issues/99mar/marketgod.htm.
4. Jeffrey Sachs, *Common Wealth,* Kindle location 957.
5. Daniel Gross, *Dumb Money* (New York: Simon & Schuster, 2009), Kindle location 116.

6. Quotes from Julie Bosman, "Newly Poor Swell Lines at Foodbanks," *The New York Times,* February 19, 2009.
7. Ibid.
8. As quoted by Charles Murray in "Virtue in a Free Society," http:// www.aei.org/issue/11107.
9. Adam Smith, *An Inquiry into the Nature and Causes of the Wealth of Nations,* Kindle location 6711.
10. Harvey Cox, "The Market as God."
11. Psalm 24:1 KJV.

CHAPTER 3: GREED IS GOOD

1. Robert Frank, *Richistan: A Journey Through the American Wealth Boom and the Lives of the New Rich* (New York: Random House, 2007).
2. Frank, *Richistan,* Kindle location 1577.
3. Louise Story, "Home Equity Frenzy Was a Bank Ad Come True," *New York Times,* August 14, 2008, http://www.nytimes.com/2008/08/15/ business/15sell.html#/from/5.
4. Jeane M. Twenge, Ph.D., and W. Keith Campbell, Ph.D., *The Narcissism Epidemic* (New York: Simon & Schuster, 2009), Kindle location 607.
5. Frank, *Richistan,* Kindle location 1552.
6. Matthew 6:19–21 NLT.

CHAPTER 4: IT'S ALL ABOUT ME

1. "Greenspan Testimony on Sources of Financial Crisis," WSJ Blogs, Real Time Economics, October 23, 2008, http://blogs.wsj.com/ economics/2008/10/23/greenspan-testimony-on-sources-of-financial -crisis/.
2. http://oversight.house.gov/documents/20081024163819.pdf.
3. Neil Irwin and Amit R. Paley, "Greenspan Says He Was Wrong on Regulation," *Washington Post,* October 24, 2008, http://www .washingtonpost.com/wp-dyn/content/article/2008/10/23/AR2008 102300193.html.
4. www.facebook.com/press.

5. http://www.cameraguild.com/news/genindustry/070125_Reality -TV.html.

6. Lia Miller, "So Many Paparazzi, So Few Coveted Shots," *New York Times,* May 9, 2005, http://www.nytimes.com/2005/05/09/business/media/09tabloid.html.

7. Lacey Rose, "The Most Expensive Celebrity Photos," Forbes.com, July 18, 2007, http://www.forbes.com/2007/07/17/celebrities_photo journalism-magazines-biz-media-cx_lr_0718celebphotos.html.

8. John M. Darley and C. Daniel Batson, "From Jerusalem to Jericho: A Study of Situation and Dispositional Variables in Helping Behavior," http://www.aug.edu/sociology/Jerusalem.htm.

9. http://www.docshop.com/2007/10/20/mommy-makeover-plastic -surgery-on-the-rise/.

10. http://kidshealth.org/teen/your_body/beautiful/plastic_surgery.html#; http://www.plasticsurgery.org/Media/stats/2008-teen-cosmetic-surgery -minimally-invasive.pdf.

11. Twenge and Campbell, *The Narcissism Epidemic,* Kindle location 201.

12. Atul Gawande, "Hellhole," *New Yorker,* March 30, 2009, http://www .newyorker.com/reporting/2009/03/30/090330fa_fact_gawande.

13. Gawande, "Hellhole."

CHAPTER 5: I WANT IT NOW

1. Ben Woolsey and Matt Schulz, "Credit card statistics, industry facts, debt statistics," http://www.creditcards.com/credit-card-news/credit _card_industry_facts_personal_debt_statistics_1276.php.

2. Frank, *Richistan,* Kindle location 1927.

3. Amy Schoenfeld and Matthew Bloch, "The American Way of Debt," n.d., http://nytimes.com/interactive/2008/07/20/business/20debt_trap .html#section 3/2.

4. Kristin Kovner, "10 Things Your College Student Won't Tell You," May 2009, http://www.smartmoney.com/spending/rip-offs/10-things -your-college-student-wont-tell-you-19913/?page=2.

5. Greg Anrig, "Who Strangled the FDA?," http://www.prospect.org/cs/ articles?article=who_strangled_the_fda.

6. Abbie Boudreau and Scott Bronstein, "Poor Oversight Fueled Salmo-

nella Outbreak, Experts Say," http://www.cnn.com/2009/HEALTH/ 02/05/peanut.recall/.

7. Bret Schulte, "Outlawing Text Messaging While Driving," *U.S.News & World Report,* February 11, 2008, http://www.usnews.com/articles/ news/national/2008/02/11/outlawing-text-messaging-while-driving .html.

8. Michael Austin, "Texting While Driving: How Dangerous Is It?," *Car and Driver,* June 2009, http://www.caranddriver.com/features/09q2/ texting_while_driving_how_dangerous_is_it-feature.

9. Schulte, "Outlawing Text Messaging."

10. Austin, "Texting While Driving."

11. Jad Mouawad and Kate Galbraith, "Plugged-in Age Feeds a Hunger for Electricity," *New York Times,* September 19, 2009-http://www .nytimes.com/2009/09/20/business/energy-environment/20efficiency .html?_r=1&th&emc=th.

12. "Mountaintop Removal Coal Mining," Appalachian Voices, http:// www.appvoices.org/index.php?/site/mtr_overview.

13. Michael S. Rosenthal, "Left in the Flat-Screen Dust," *Washington Post,* September 19, 2009, http://www.washingtonpost.com/wp-dyn/con tent/article/2009/09/18/AR2009091803711.html.

14. http://www.processor.com/editorial/article.asp?article=articles%2Fp 3105%2F3 0p05%2F30p05%2F30p05.asp.

15. Rhett Butler, "Deforestation in the Amazon," http://www.mongabay .com/brazil.html.

16. http://creativecitizen.com/solutions/232-Don-t-Eat-Beef.

17. Romans 8:19–23.

CHAPTER 6: WHEN THE GAPS GET TOO BIG

1. http://financialservices.house.gov/ExecCompvsWorkers.html.

2. Sarah Anderson, et al., "America's Bailout Barons," September 2009, Institute for Policy Studies, http://www.ips-dc.org/reports/executive _excess_2009

3. Robert Reich, *Supercapitalism: The Transformation of Business, Democracy, and Everyday Life* (New York: Knopf, 2007), Kindle location 611.

4. Paul Krugman, *The Conscience of a Liberal* (New York: Norton, 2007), Kindle location 1069.

5. Krugman, *Conscience of a Liberal,* Kindle location 1873.

6. Reich, *Supercapitalism,* Kindle location 1794.
7. Reich, *Supercapitalism,* Kindle location 1884.
8. http://www.forbes.com/lists/2007/12/lead_07ceos_Angelo-R-Mozilo_7G33.html.
9. http://www.forbes.com/lists/2007/12/lead_07ceos_Steven-P-Jobs_HEDB.html.
10. "The Quiet Coup," Atlantic, http://www.theatlantic.com/doc/200905/imf-advice/3.
11. Reich, *Supercapitalism,* Kindle location 1894.
12. Ibid.
13. Krugman, *Conscience of a Liberal,* Kindle location 1873.
14. Arloc Sherman, "Income Inequality Hits Record Levels," Center on Budget and Policy Priorities, December 14, 2007, http://www.cbpp.org/cms/?fa=view&id=917.
15. Krugman, *Conscience of a Liberal,* Kindle location 1670.
16. Reich, *Supercapitalism,* Kindle location 1714.
17. Krugman, *Conscience of a Liberal,* Kindle location 1743.
18. Krugman, *Conscience of a Liberal,* Kindle location 3461.
19. Emmanuel Saez, "Striking It Richer: The Evolution of Top Incomes in the United States," August 5, 2009, http://elsa.berkeley.edu/~saez/saez-UStopincomes-2007.pdf.
20. http://www.federalreserve.gov/Pubs/feds/2009/200913/200913abs.html.
21. "Wealth in the United States: How Concentrated?," http://www.toomuchonline.org/inequality.html.
22. Ecclesiastes 9:1 NIV.

CHAPTER 7: ON LISTENING TO CANARIES

1. Acts 2:44–45 NIV.
2. Aristides, *Apology,* 15.
3. http://etext.virginia.edu/jefferson/quotations/jeff1550.htm.
4. http://press-pubs.uchicago.edu/founders/documents/v1ch15s50.html.
5. http://www.thomaspaine.org/Archives/agjst.html.
6. http://www.demos.org/inequality/quotes.cfm.
7. http://www.pm.gov.au/node/6201.

CHAPTER 8: ENOUGH IS ENOUGH

1. Matthew 6:25–29 NIV.
2. Matthew 6:31–34.
3. PNC Advisors Wealth and Values Survey 2005, http://www2.prnews wire.com/cgi-bin/mincro_stories.pl?ACCT=701257&TICK=PNC& STORY=/www/story/01–10–2005/0002814679&EDATE=Jan+10, +2005.
4. Frank, *Richistan,* Kindle location 801.
5. Jonathan Sacks, *The Dignity of Difference* (New York: Continuum, 2002), 32.
6. Sacks, *Dignity of Difference,* 33.
7. Shaila Dewan, "Extravagance Has Its Limits As Belt-Tightening Trickles Up," *New York Times,* March 9, 2009, http://www.nytimes.com/2009/03/10/us/10reset.html?scp=1&sq=%22Carol%20Morgan%22&st=cse.
8. Dewan, "Extravagance Has Its Limits."
9. Clement of Alexandria, *Early Church Fathers,* 51.
10. Augustine, *Early Church Fathers,* 55.
11. Chrysostom, *Early Church Fathers,* 50.
12. Pelagian Tract, *Early Church Fathers,* 54.
13. "Reverend Billy's Bailout," *Wall Street Journal,* April 16, 2009, http://online.wsj.com/article/SB123982723145222287.html.
14. Frank Greve, "America's Poor Are Its Most Generous Givers," McClatchy.com, May 19, 2009, http://www.mcclatchydc.com/226/story/68456.html.
15. "Giving in Tough Times," IndependentSector.com, 2009, http://www.independentsector.org/programs/research/toughtimes.html.
16. Greve, "America's Poor."

CHAPTER 9: WE'RE IN IT TOGETHER

1. https://www.hcsbonline.com.
2. "Small Town Banks Dull but Profitable," *San Francisco Sentinel,* October 20, 2009, http://www.sanfranciscosentinel.com/?p=26395.
3. Samuel G. Freedman, "A Hometown Bank Heeds a Call to Serve Its Islamic Clients," *New York Times,* March 6, 2009, http://www.nytimes.com/2009/03/07/us/07religion.html.

4. Lillian Kwon, "More Children Forced into Labor Amid Economic Crisis," Christian Post, http://www.christianpost.com/article/2009 0516/more-children-forced-into-labor-amid-economic-crisis/index .html.

5. John Thavis, "Global Food Crisis Caused by Selfishness, Speculation, Says Pope," Catholic News Service, October 16, 2008, http://www .catholicnews.com/data/stories/cns/0805262.htm.

CHAPTER 10: THE SEVENTH-GENERATION MIND-SET

1. Elizabeth Palmberg, "The Notorious I.B.G.," www.godspolitics.com, September 15, 2009.

2. Genesis 2:2–3.

3. Ronald Wright, *A Short History of Progress* (New York: Carroll & Graf, 2005).

4. Thomas Friedman, "The Inflection Is Near," *New York Times,* March 7, 2009.

5. http://www.ipcc.ch/pdf/assessment-report/ar4/syr/ar4_syr_spm.pdf.

6. https://www.vts.edu/ftpimages/95/misc/misc_62950.pdf.

7. http://faithinpubliclife.org/content/press/2009/05/us_reps_people _of_faith_ want_a_1.html.

CHAPTER 11: THE CLEAN-ENERGY ECONOMY CONVERSION

1. David Owen, "Economy vs. Environment," *New Yorker,* March 30, 2009, http://www.newyorker.com/talk/comment/2009/03/30/090330 taco_talk_owen.

2. Elisabeth Rosenthal, "In German Suburb, Life Goes On Without Cars," *New York Times,* May 11, 2009, http://www.nytimes.com/ 2009/05/12/science/earth/12suburb.html.

3. Rosenthal, "In German Suburb."

4. "Share My Ride," *New York Times,* March 5, 2009, http://www .nytimes.com/2009/03/08/magazine/08Zipcar-t.html?pagewanted=3.

5. http://financecareers.about.com/b/2008/05/13/finance-and-the-harvard -grad.htm.

6. All this information comes from Thomas Friedman, *Hot, Flat, and Crowded* (New York: Farrar, Straus, 2008).
7. http://www.greenchange.org/article.php?id=4434.
8. http://kansasipl.org/2009/06/wichita-eagle-op-ed-people-of-faith-must-care-for-creation/.

CHAPTER 12: THE FAMILY MATTERS CULTURE

1. Jeanne Sahadi, "Who Gets the Most (and Least) Vacation," CNN Money.com, June 14, 2007,http://money.cnn.com/2007/06/12/pf/vacation_days_worldwide/.
2. http://www.dol.gov/esa/whd/fmla/.
3. http://en.wikipedia.org/wiki/Parental_leave.
4. Thomas Merton, "Letter to a Young Activist," *The Hidden Ground of Love* (New York: Farrar, Straus, 1985).

CHAPTER 13: THE MEANING OF WORK AND THE ETHIC OF SERVICE

1. Isaiah 65:22–23.
2. Psalm 128:2.
3. Sacks, *Dignity of Difference*, 94.
4. http://financecareers.about.com/b/2008/05/13/finance-and-the-harvard-grad.htm.
5. Adam Smith, *The Theory of Moral Sentiments,* Kindle location 1000.
6. http://www.nationalservice.gov/about/newsroom/releases_detail.asp?tbl_pr_id=1289.

CHAPTER 14: REGAINING OUR BALANCE

1. All Blank's quotes are taken from this interview: http://www.americanprogress.org/issues/2009/04/blank_interview.html.
2. http://www.reason.com/news/show/118175.html.
3. Reich, *Supercapitalism* loc 3313–16.
4. http://www.eoionline.org/minimum_wage/.

5. Romans 13:3–4.
6. Reich, *Supercapitalism*, Kindle location 4420.

CHAPTER 15: THE PARABLE OF DETROIT AND THE GREEN SHOOTS OF HOPE

1. Judy Keen, "Detroit Community Groups Work for City's New Glory Days," *USA Today*, May 29, 2009.
2. http://blogs.abcnews.com/theworldnewser/2009/08/unemployment-in-detroit-climbs-to-289.html.
3. http://www.mlive.com/news/detroit/index.ssf/2009/08/detroit_unemployment_rises_to.html.
4. Nick Bunkley, "Detroit Churches Pray for 'God's Bailout,'" *New York Times*, December 7, 2008.
5. Keen, "Detroit Community Groups Work for City's New Glory Days."
6. http://www.sojo.net/index.cfm?action-agazine.article&issue=soj0905&article =resurrection-city.
7. Keen, "Detroit Community Groups Work for City's New Glory Days."
8. http://208.176.52.77/content/upload/AssetMgmt/Site/HOUSING/Jan09stats.pdf.
9. Toby Barlow, "For Sale: The $100 House," *New York Times*, March 7, 2009.
10. Nehemiah 2:17–18.
11. Nehemiah 4:14.
12. Lee Jenkins, "Tigertown," *Sports Illustrated*, September 28, 2009.

CHAPTER 16: A BAD MORALITY PLAY

1. Transcribed from http://www.breitbart.tv/mad-money-host-cramer-likens-bonus-outrage-to-lenin-in-1917/.
2. http://www.nytimes.com/2009/10/13/business/economy/13sorkin.html
3. http://blogs.wsj.com/deals/2009/07/30/bank-of-america-the-cuomo-reports-bonus_breakdown/http://blogs.wsj.com/deals/2009/07/30/citigroup-the-cuomo-reports-bonus-breakdown/

4. http://www.bloomberg.com/apps/news?pid=20601087&sid=aJ8HPm
   NUfchg
5. http://dyn.politico.com/printstory.cfm?uuid=69E52D28–18FE-70B2
   -A852F629D4620071

READING GROUP
GUIDE

This reading group guide for *Rediscovering Values* includes an introduction, discussion questions, ideas for enhancing your book club, and a Q&A with author Jim Wallis. The suggested questions are intended to help your reading group find new and interesting angles and topics for your discussion. We hope that these ideas will enrich your conversation and increase your enjoyment of the book.

INTRODUCTION

Part treatise, part blueprint for personal and economic recovery and sustainability, and part meditation on America's shifting moral center, *Rediscovering Values* features *New York Times* bestselling author and public theologian Jim Wallis at his best.

With the invisible hand of the market reaching a God-like status during the economic boom of the past decade, many Americans have been misdirecting their faith and have allowed greed and financial prospects to guide them. But, maintains Wallis, it is in times of crises where opportunities for change arise. Rather than letting the events of the Great Recession defeat us, Wallis urges Americans to recalibrate their lives, creating a moral compass for the new economy. The old maxims that got us into this mess were greed is good, it's all about me, and I want it now. It's time to replace those misguided principles with some of our oldest and best values—enough is enough, we're in this together, and we must consider how our decisions will affect the next seven generations. Remembering these lessons will not only help us keep afloat during the Great Recession, but will keep us from falling victim to the traps that led us here in the first place. Wallis calls for a conversion to take place—an economic and spiritual conversion that extends from Wall Street to Main Street to Your Street.

QUESTIONS FOR DISCUSSION

1. One of the most poignant moments of the book occurs early on as Wallis describes his experience reciting Gandhi's Seven Deadly Social Sins to a room full of world business leaders (p. 6). Discuss these seven pillars of wisdom. How can they be applied to economics? Did the violation of any of these social contracts lead directly or indirectly to the Great Recession?

2. Wallis uses several biblical passages to illustrate that many of our current financial and moral dilemmas are as old as history. Most notably, the narrative of the Money Changers (p. 16), the parable of the Golden Calf (p. 26), and the parable of the Good Samaritan (p. 58). Which of these passages of scripture spoke to you the most? Which do you think is most directly applicable to the Great Recession?

3. Debt is a tool, Wallis argues, that can help achieve goals and dreams but can also be seductive and destructive. What lessons can we learn from the Great Recession about how debt is used and abused?

4. "New Old Values" (p. 89) is an important concept to grasp while trying to avoid falling back into the same old pre-recession habits. What new old values can you remember from your childhood? Are there any new old values that you think will prove vital to our nation's economic recovery?

5. One of the telltale signs of a coming economic downturn, Wallis notes, is a period of opulent spending and conspicuous consumption that precedes a crash. Is it more difficult to keep a moral compass during times of great economic growth or during the financial struggles of a recession?

6. Wallis draws several parallels between the Great Depression and the Great Recession. The Great Depression left an indelible mark on the generation who experienced it. What values do we generally associate with Americans who lived through this difficult time? Are those values still applicable today?

7. With the unemployment rate rising and the lingering effects of our recession becoming even more visible, Wallis observes that the poor are now our neighbors and friends, not just an unseen subsection of the population. Is it immoral for us to ignore poverty in America until it directly affects us?

8. "The Great Lie" in chapter 6 is that wealth is God's reward for spiritual righteousness, and that the poor are being punished for their moral depravity. Do you agree that this is simply a myth? Why or why not?

9. God's economy, Wallis says, is ruled by the principle "there *is* enough, if we *share* it" (p. 38), yet the gap between rich and poor in the world continues to widen. Are people with a lot of money morally obligated to share their wealth?

10. Do you think that government initiatives to temper extreme disparities are an un-American approach to our economic disparities? Wallis argues that the gap between rich and poor will continuously widen if there is no intervention for the common good. Do you agree?

11. Wallis is careful to distinguish between blind rage and effective anger. Rage is a reaction, whereas effective anger comes with a vision. Are there other emotions and feelings that can be harnessed and put to good use as we recover from the recession?

12. Wallis chooses to use the word *conversion* to describe the change that America needs. What does conversion mean when applied to personal behavior, the economy, and the whole of society? Do you think an overhaul of values in American society can be an interfaith effort, or will crisis drive us further apart?

13. After reading this book, what values do you think are the most important to rediscover? What should be the values on Wall Street, Main Street, and Your Street?

ENHANCE YOUR BOOK CLUB

1. Pick up a copy of *Sojourners,* the magazine founded by Jim Wallis. This Washington D.C.–based periodical is full of stories that expand upon current events touched upon in this book. You can easily enhance your discussions on topics such as health care and the emerging green economy by revisiting these hot-button issues every month.

2. How do you stack up to the world's richest? You'd be surprised. Go to the Global Rich List recommended on page 88 of the book to get some perspective on America's incredible standard of living (www.globalrichlist.com). Put your annual salary to the test: a modest $25,000 a year would put you in the top 10 percent of the world's richest people!

3. As Wallis notes, "While you can read this book on your own, you can't live it on your own." Put your own thoughts and ideas into action by joining the discussion online at www.rediscoveringvalues.org. The fight against poverty and economic and social injustice in America and worldwide cannot be won alone.

4. In the book, Wallis points out that before Adam Smith wrote his famous treaty on economics, he wrote about ethics

and morality. In fact, it seems that morality and economics are inextricably linked. Ayn Rand, a strong proponent of free-market ideology, argued that selfishness is a virtue while Wallis argues that it is a vice. Do you think you can separate economics and morality? Is selfishness a virtue or is it a vice?

5. Everyone has had their own personal experiences with the Great Recession. Take turns sharing a story that encapsulates what you think makes this time in American history unique. Are you optimistic that we will come out of this a better nation, or are we bound to repeat the mistakes of the past?

A CONVERSATION WITH JIM WALLIS

1. Did you always envision writing a book centered on economics, or was the project a response to our current financial climate and the new challenges America faces as a result?

I actually had about five other book ideas and not a single one of them had this kind of focus on economics. I began to tell the story about the World Economic Forum, which I write about in the introduction, and I would get an overwhelming response. After one talk that included "Sunday School with Jon Stewart" and the story of the five loaves and two fish, my special assistant and communication manager, Tim King, told me, "Jim, there is a book in that sermon!" He would sit in the crowd while I preached, and he would describe the looks of hope on people's faces when they heard about the idea of "God's Economy" and using the crisis as an opportunity to relearn old lessons. We started working on an outline and researching soon after that.

2. **You pinpoint the green revolution and the movement toward clean energy as a key to our economic and moral recovery. Do you think that the moral benefits of pursuing clean energy are sufficient to stave off any short-term financial disincentives? Do you envision that moral profits and losses will ever play a bigger role than financial profits and losses in our decision making?**

As evidenced at the World Economic Forum, more and more business leaders are beginning to think in terms of more than just a financial bottom line. They are also thinking about community impact and environmental stability as bottom lines, and they are learning that you can both do good and do well. It's true that a movement towards a green economy might make the cost of filling up your car go up a bit, but that also means more jobs for people in our country to make sure we have alternative energy resources. Investing in public transportation might mean a good chunk of change, but it also means that more kids living in the city can leave their inhalers at home because the air they are breathing is cleaner. Putting money into weatherizing your home and getting energy efficient appliances means an investment now with savings for years to come. If your mind-set stays "I want it now," then a green revolution makes little sense; but if you care about your kids and have a seventh-generation mind-set, then you have both a moral and an economic imperative.

3. **You have stated publicly many times that you believe religion does not have a monopoly on morality, and yet you are a very prominent Christian leader. Is it difficult to bridge the gap between faiths while simultaneously maintaining a strong Christian belief yourself?**

I work hard to bridge the gaps between people of other faiths exactly because of how strongly I hold my own Christian beliefs. Working with people who believe differently than I do in no way makes me give up any of the unique truth claims that I hold as a follower of Christ. Globally, I have over one billion Muslim neighbors; I can either be an agent of peace, as Jesus told his disciples to be, or I can be an agent for conflict and violence. I choose peace. Some of my nearest and dearest friends—friends whom I would trust with my life—claim no particular faith at all. But when it comes to things like concern for the poor, hope for peace, and preservation of the environment, I sometimes find I have more things in common with them than with some Christians I know.

4. **With so much corruption in the financial sector coming to light during the recession, it is impossible to dismiss the notion that wealth corrupts. With this in mind, would you advise young men and women to steer away from careers in finance or challenge them to transform the industry while keeping both feet firmly grounded?**

Yes and yes. As I mention in the book, just a few years ago an inordinate amount of Harvard students were planning on going into the financial services industry. I believe the primary motivation was not so they could help small business grow through loans or because they wanted to ensure that couples could retire comfortably or that families could save for college, but because it seemed like the quickest way to make some big money. Many of the practices of our financial system have been shown to be a kind of upscale, dangerous casino with a few big firms having the game rigged in their favor. So I certainly hope a lot more young people are considering careers of service and producing real goods and services, but I also hope that those young people who get into the financial industry do it with a deep ethical commitment to providing real services and not just Wall Street roulette.

5. You are friends with President Obama and famously defended his faith after James Dobson called it into question leading up to the 2008 presidential election. Do you think that President Obama has been guided by his faith while dealing with the financial crisis? What effect do you think faith-based policy can have on the American economy?

Well, part of my criticism of James Dobson was that he publicly judged the state of another person's faith. The president has had a lot of difficult decisions in front of him, and I am not the ultimate judge of whether or not he is faithful. But, as you can see, especially in the final section of the book, I have not been impressed with quite a few economic decisions that have been made, some under the Bush administration and some under the Obama administration. We have been seeing a lot of Band-Aids but not a lot of the deeper restructuring I think we need. There are two concepts, both of which I touch on in the book, that offer some hopeful faith-based policy for the American economy. First, all of the Abrahamic religions strongly condemn "usury," which is interpreted as excessive interest on loans or, sometimes, as any interest at all. I think our country needs to crack down on predatory lending where lenders charge huge amounts of interest and often include fine print or use deceptive advertising to trap people in debt. From mortgage scams to "payday lending" shops that seem to be on every street corner of our cities, we need to start cracking down on usury. Second, our country is often a "buyer beware" kind of place, and anything goes as long as the seller can get away with it. In the Old Testament, especially, we see a lot of talk about the moral responsibility that merchants have not only to their customers but to society at large.

6. **You infuse your writing with popular culture references and have appeared multiple times on *The Daily Show* and other popular television shows. Has this kind of exposure helped you reach a younger audience? How receptive are younger generations to your message?**

When I go on the road to speak, half of my audiences are under thirty. Young people are often fascinated by Jesus and what he stood for, but just can't stand the Christians they often see on TV. Time after time I hear stories of young people who return to their faith or find it for the first time because they want to follow after the Jesus who proclaimed good news to the poor, freedom for the oppressed, and the year of jubilee! If you stop buy the Sojourners offices in D.C. and meet some of my staff, you will meet a group of some of the smartest, most dedicated young Christians in the country.

7. **You speak very fondly of your experiences coaching both of your sons' Little League Baseball teams. Professional sports, however, have become almost synonymous with overspending and price gouging. How can we account for the disconnect between the potential sports has to teach valuable lessons and the economic realities of professional sports in America?**

Not just price gouging, but have you seen the commercials that are on during sports games! I have to cover up my kids eyes and block their ears. For some baseball games, I swear there are more commercials for the little blue pill than there are hits. With the big contracts and some of the wild adventures of sports superstars, I'm pretty convinced that many of them have forgotten the lessons of Little League.

8. **You make an interesting observation that celebrities have replaced heroes in American culture and that their inevitable status as role models causes a trickle-down effect of bad values. Who do you think are the modern-day heroes in American culture? Who were yours growing up?**

I tell the story in the book about my son Luke's fifth-grade assignment to find and research a "hero" and write an essay about him or her. He found lots of them, including Desmond Tutu, Martin Luther King Jr., Bono, environmental activists, and of course, Lebron James!

9. **How does being from Detroit change the way you approach writing and talking about the Great Recession? Does it make it more difficult for you personally to transform blind rage into effective anger?**

Detroit has become a parable in this Great Recession—as I write about in the book. My hometown is an example of the social contract that has been broken, and the suffering that has caused. But it also points to the power of resilience and hope.

10. **In American politics, religious faith has become an unavoidable component of a candidate's ultimate success or**

failure. Do you eventually see faith playing a similar role in finance as it becomes a more transparent and increasingly regulated industry?

If faith doesn't change how a political leader does politics or how a business leader does business or how we all do what we do—then it doesn't mean very much.

11. **Would you say that economic recovery is inevitable if moral recovery is achieved?**

What I am saying is that we won't have or be able to sustain a true economic recovery without a moral recovery. What we need is not to go back to normal: we need a new normal.

12. **Now that you have tackled the intersection of economics and morality, what are some of the topics that intrigue you going forward? Are there any emerging issues that you're itching to write about?**

I want to write a book about Gandhi's Seven Deadly Social Sins that I just mention in this book, because they are so morally diagnostic of our present situation. And I want to write a book about my boy's prayers and one on the lessons of life you can learn from baseball!

sojourners

Faith in Action for Social Justice

 **JIM WALLIS** is the founder and executive director of **Sojourners**, a Christian organization whose mission is to articulate the biblical call to social justice, inspiring hope and building a movement to transform individuals, communities, the church, and the world.

More from Sojourners and Jim Wallis

Want to learn more about how your faith can change the things that really matter? Visit **www.sojo.net** to find out how you can put your faith into action:

- Sign up for SojoMail, a free weekly e-zine.

- Take action online for justice.

- Get a free trial issue of *Sojourners* magazine.

- Search for a church near you.

- Register for upcoming events and trainings.

- Apply to become a Sojourners intern.

- Read the God's Politics blog (www.godspolitics.com) for daily commentary by Jim Wallis and friends.

- Make a donation and invest in the movement for social justice.

For more information, visit **www.sojo.net** or contact:

sojourners

3333 14th St. NW, Suite 200, Washington, DC 20010 USA
Phone: (202) 328-8842 or 1-800-714-7474
E-mail: sojourners@sojo.net